PICTORIAL ART QUILT
GUIDEBOOK
Secrets to Capturing Your Photos in Fabric

LENI LEVENSON WIENER

Text copyright © 2014 by Leni Levenson Wiener

Photography and Artwork copyright © 2014 by C&T Publishing, Inc.

Publisher: Amy Marson

Creative Director: Gailen Runge

Art Director: Kristy Zacharias

Editor: Liz Aneloski

Technical Editors: Nanette S. Zeller and Gailen Runge

Cover Designer: April Mostek

Book Designer: Christina Jarumay Fox

Production Coordinator: Rue Flaherty

Production Editor: Alice Mace Nakanishi

Illustrator: Jenny Davis

Photo Assistant: Mary Peyton Peppo

Style photography by Nissa Brehmer and instructional photography by Diane Pedersen, unless otherwise noted

Published by C&T Publishing, Inc., P.O. Box 1456, Lafayette, CA 94549

Library of Congress Cataloging-in-Publication Data

Wiener, Leni Levenson.

 Pictorial art quilt guidebook : secrets to capturing your photos in fabric / Leni Levenson Wiener.

   pages cm.

 ISBN 978-1-60705-744-4 (soft cover)

1. Art quilts. 2. Photography. I. Title.

 TT772.W538 2014

 746.46022'2--dc23

                         2013037426

Printed in the USA

10 9 8 7 6 5

ACKNOWLEDGMENTS

I would like to thank the following fabric companies for their generosity in providing many of the fabrics used in this book. Please look for their gorgeous fabric selections at your local fabric store:

Alexander Henry

Andover Fabrics

Dear Stella Fabrics

Michael Miller Fabrics

P&B Textiles

Robert Kaufman Co.

Timeless Treasure Fabric

Westminster Fabrics / FreeSpirit

In addition, I would like to thank the team at C&T for their assistance and guidance throughout the preparation of this book, and the following people for the use of their beautiful photographs as inspiration for some of the art quilts contained in this book:

Linda Beach

Aaron Epstein

Lin Hsin-Chen

Sue Freebern

Steve McCurry / Magnum Photos

CONTENTS

INTRODUCTION

I like to describe what I do as fabric collage. For many years, photographs have been the starting point for my art quilts. I love translating a photo into fabric, adding layers of complexity using color and pattern. Starting with a photo frees me from having to figure out the proportions, the perspective, and where the light and shadows will be. All the information I need is there for me, and when in doubt—those times when my brain says, "No, that wouldn't look like that"—my eyes know for sure. That is why I always tell my students, "Use your eyes, not your brain." The photo—and the working pattern you make from it—are your road map to a successful art quilt.

I start by making a pattern from the photo using a computer and printing the pattern in the full size of my final art quilt. I trace each section onto freezer paper, lay it on the fabric, press, and cut. Putting the art quilt together is like fitting pieces into a puzzle—or painting by number. When everything is in place, I sew the pieces, and my masterpiece is done.

This book has been separated into three sections. In the first section, you will learn about color, value, and print scale. I will teach you how to use color to achieve the look you want, without being a slave to the color wheel, which most people find so frustrating. You will learn the importance of value and how to collect fabrics that will serve you well as you make art quilts on your own.

In the second section, we will make an art quilt together, step by step. It is just like being at one of my workshops, but in your own home.

Finally, the last section of the book will give you easy and practical ways to approach common elements in art quilts—elements like trees and water, and tricks to do faces in fabric. I will show you how to create each of these elements using one fabric, two fabrics, or three or more fabrics for an explosion of color and pattern. After you know how to do this, you will have the tools to confidently turn any photo into an art quilt.

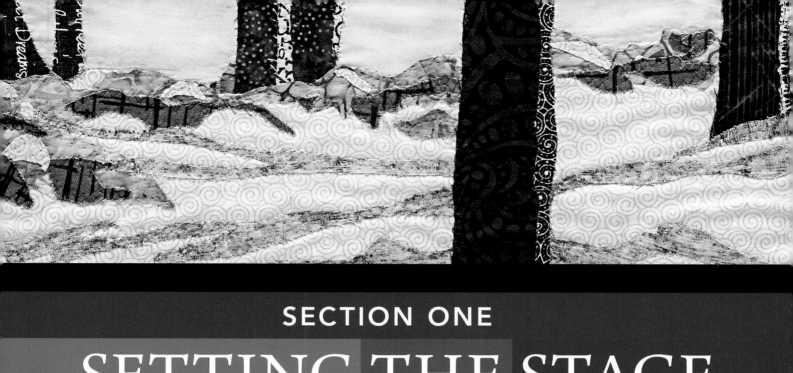

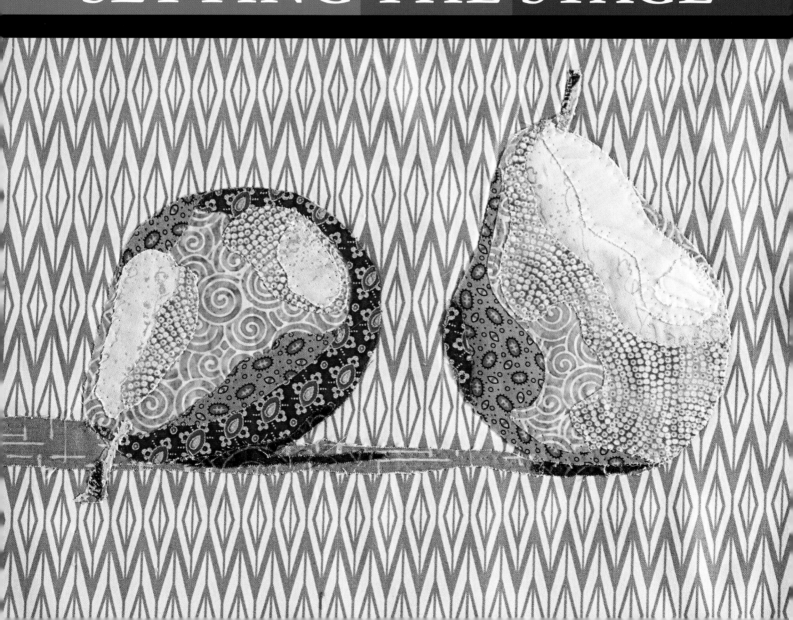

DEMYSTIFYING COLOR

All You Need to Know about Color

Throw away that color wheel; here is all you need to know about color.

Color is one of the most important building blocks in designing an art quilt. Color can set the tone of your work, evoke a mood, create depth and distance, and establish a focal point. This is true not just for quilts but for clothing, home decorating—anywhere color is used. The world is filled with colors, and each and every one elicits a feeling in humans. Understanding how will allow you to use color as a tool to achieve the feeling you want in your art quilt.

I don't use a color wheel—I don't even own one. You do not need to own one, use one, or think about one. Instead, learning the makeup of colors will help you to understand their impact and their relationships to each other, so you can make good color decisions while you work.

A color wheel simply arranges colors in order between the primaries and opposite their complements. The problem with using a color wheel is that it shows you solid colors—usually in only one value. The color wheel becomes very confusing when you try to use it to look for fabrics. Learning the makeup of the color you are considering is more effective in knowing how to use it. Eventually, with practice, this becomes second nature and you will know instantly what you need in order to achieve the look you want.

Color Basics

Let us start with the basics. There are three primary colors. You have certainly heard this before, but what exactly does it mean? It is simple. There are only three colors from which all other colors are made.

The three primary colors are red, blue, and yellow. If you come to understand these three colors, you will come to understand the *recipes* used for the creation of all other colors, and how and why they relate to each other.

You may be thinking that black and white are also primary colors. Technically, they are not colors at all—black is the absence of all color and white is the presence of all color. Practically, when black is added to any color, the color gets darker. The more black you add, the darker the color. This is called a *shade*.

When white is added to any color, it gets lighter. The more white you add, the lighter the color. This is called a *tint*. (To be honest, these are not terms you need to know to understand how to use color for the results you want, but it will either impress your friends at your next dinner party or stop the conversation altogether—probably the latter.)

Think about paint. If you have a dab of red paint and add a little white, it becomes dark pink; a little more white and the pink gets lighter. Keep adding white to the red, and the pink will get lighter and lighter until it is almost white.

The same is true of black. Add a bit of black paint to your red and it becomes a darker red. The more black paint you add, the darker the red becomes until it is almost black itself. When you add both black and white, the resulting color appears "dusty" or more subdued.

So let's begin by looking at the three primary colors: red, blue, and yellow.

Name: **RED**	*Name:* **BLUE**	*Name:* **YELLOW**
Recipe: Red is one of the three primary colors.	*Recipe:* Blue is one of the three primary colors.	*Recipe:* Yellow is one of the three primary colors.
Personality: Bold, fiery, passionate	*Personality:* Cool, calm	*Personality:* Cheerful, sunny
Plays well with: Oranges and purples	*Plays well with:* Greens and purples	*Plays well with:* Oranges and greens
Opposite: Green	*Opposite:* Orange	*Opposite:* Purple
Temperature: Hot	*Temperature:* Cool to cold	*Temperature:* Warm

Color Recipes

Remember back in preschool when you got your hands in the finger paint? You learned the first basic recipes for colors when you started moving your fingers around the paper.

Red + yellow = orange

Red + blue = purple

Blue + yellow = green

When you swirled the paint around and the red, yellow, and blue mixed together, you got brown.

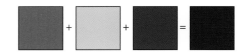

Color Temperature

Color temperature refers to the way the color is perceived and sets the **mood** of an artwork.

Blues and greens are cool colors, the colors of water and plants. These colors will set a restful and serene mood.

Reds and oranges are warm colors, the colors of fire and heat, and will set a mood in your artwork that is dynamic and exciting.

Purple can play on either team, as it is the result of mixing red (warm) and blue (cool). Depending on their recipe, purples tend to be either warmer or cooler.

Using only primary colors will appear childlike and straightforward.

Using soft, light pastel colors (colors with white added) will set a gentle mood.

Dusty colors (colors to which both black and white are added) appear romantic and antique.

Colors in *Out in the Cold* give the sense that this is a cold, damp day.

Colors used in *Parrot* are warm and tropical.

Complementary Colors

This leads us to the principle of **complementary colors**. Technically, complementary means colors opposite each other on the color wheel. They fight for attention, which can create interesting visual excitement. But, you do not need a color wheel to understand and use complements in your work. Those basic recipes for color are all you need to know, starting with the primaries—red, blue, and yellow.

If you mix blue and yellow, the result is **green**. The remaining primary is **red**, the complement of green.

Combine yellow and red to make **orange;** its complement is the remaining primary—**blue**.

Finally, mix blue and red to make **purple;** the remaining primary is **yellow**, the complement of purple.

Here are some examples of complementary colors in fabric.

 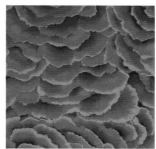

Green and red

 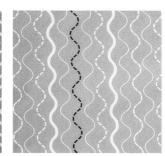

Orange and blue

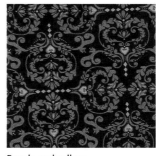 

Purple and yellow

To find the complement to more complex colors, you need to learn to determine the recipe of a color.

Take the example of teal. Teal is a color somewhere between blue and green. It is made by mixing blue and yellow (the recipe for true green), but when more blue is added to the mix, it becomes a bluer green, or teal. Teal itself can vary, depending on the amount of blue added to the basic green recipe. Hard to tell? Put the teal between a blue fabric and a green one. Which does it more closely resemble? That will tell you how much more blue or green is in the recipe.

Name: **TEAL**

Recipe: Blue mixed with green (green is blue mixed with yellow), roughly two parts blue to one part yellow

Personality: Like green, calm and peaceful, but not as cool as blue

Plays well with: Blues and greens

Opposite: Red orange

Temperature: Cool

If teal is a green that contains more blue than a true green, the complement will still be red (the complement of green), but a red with more orange (the complement of blue) in it.

Let's look at periwinkle. Periwinkle is a blue-purple combination—the result of mixing blue with purple (red and blue make purple). This means the complement will be an orange (complement of blue) but an orange with more yellow in it (complement of purple).

Name: **PERIWINKLE**

Recipe: Blue mixed with purple (purple is blue mixed with red), roughly two parts blue to one part red

Personality: Can be calm like a blue, but with a hint of warmth from the addition of red

Plays well with: Blues and purples

Opposite: Yellow orange

Temperature: Bridges the gap between cooler blues and neutral to warm purples

Importance of Complementary Colors

Why is it so important to establish a complement for a color?

Complementary colors can add drama to your art quilt. An artwork that is primarily blue will benefit from just a touch of orange. One that is primarily purple will be enlivened by even a spot of yellow. Making use of a complementary color scheme does not mean you must complement the colors exactly. If your colors are predominantly cool, use a touch of a warm color, and vice versa. However, using the true complement will heighten the impact.

Complementary colors in equal amounts can look jarring and jumbled, because the two colors fight for attention. By using just a small amount of a complementary color, you can direct a viewer to a focal point or other compositional element without any other visual distractions.

Establishing a **focal point** is easy using the principle of complementary color. Making an orange focal point in a background that is predominantly blue will instantly draw the viewer's eye to that part of the composition. Dispersing the complementary color along a path will create a sense of depth and dimension and "draw the eye in" to the composition.

Perhaps you want to make a change in your art quilt from the original photo using color to make one aspect more prominent. Look at my quilt *The Boy in the Banyan Tree*, for example. In the original photo, the boy is dressed in blue, and so is his grandfather. The surrounding banyan tree is a gray blue, which means the whole photo is monochromatic (meaning all one color; in this case shades of blue). I wanted to make the boy stand out as the star of the art quilt, so I dressed him in orange instead of blue—because orange is the complement of blue. Now, he is the first thing a viewer sees when looking at this quilt—he has become the focal point.

The Boy in the Banyan Tree

Original photo

Photo by author

Color Terminology

A **monochromatic** color scheme makes use of one single color in various values (see What Is Value?, page 21). It is very important in a monochromatic color combination to combine light, medium, and dark values of the color, so that the resulting work is dynamic and exciting. Without variations in value, monochromatic color schemes can appear flat and lifeless.

An **analogous** color scheme expands slightly beyond the monochromatic by adding colors that are adjacent on the color wheel. Simply stated, that generally means either a cool or warm color palette, like blue and green, green and yellow, yellow and orange, or orange and red; or one that makes the transition between warm and cool like red and purple, or purple and blue. Analogous color schemes are more varied than monochromatic ones but are still subtler than complementary color schemes.

 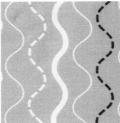   

Complementary color schemes are those that combine "opposite" colors or even just cool and warm colors together (see Complementary Colors, page 11). When using a complementary color scheme, it is important to let one dominate; if used in equal amounts the end result will be jarring. Of course, if that is the mood you wish to create, use complementary colors in similar amounts and similar values. Often just a touch of a complementary color is enough to bring a composition to life.

    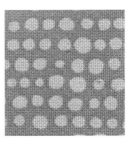

Saturation refers to the intensity of a color. Think about a dye bath. If you put white fabric into blue dye for a few minutes, the result will be a light blue. Leave it in a long time and you will have a deep, rich blue. Add gray to the color and the saturation drops immediately. Saturated colors are happy and bright; highly saturated colors in a landscape, for instance, will look tropical and sun-drenched. Grayer, less-saturated colors look soft and muted. Landscapes done in less-saturated colors give the appearance of a foggy day.

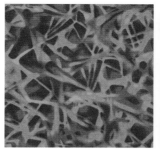

More- and less-saturated green fabrics

I used highly saturated colors in *Parrot* (full quilt on page 88).

Saturation can also create **depth and distance** in your composition. Objects in the foreground should be darker and more saturated than those that recede into the distance. In a mountain range, for example, the farther away the mountain, the lighter, cooler, and grayer the colors appear. That will mean choosing a fabric that is lighter and **dustier** (less saturated) than those in the foreground. Making a far, distant mountain dark or highly saturated will bring it forward into the front of your composition, thereby reducing the distance it appears to be from the foreground.

Detail of *Man Standing Looking at Mountain* (full quilt on page 84)

I used less-saturated colors in *Bluejay* (full quilt on page 89).

Gray, Beige, and Taupe

Gray, beige, and taupe are the problem children of the color world.

If you mix black and white in equal amounts, the resulting color is gray. Put more black in the mix and the result is dark gray; more white and it is light gray.

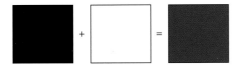

Mix all three primaries together, and the result is brown. Beige is just light brown, so adding white to the three mixed primaries creates shades of beige.

There is an annoying problem when working with gray and beige fabrics. Why do these colors always seem to have a different "agenda"? The reason is that not all grays or beiges are "clean" colors; they do not contain equal amounts of their components in their recipe. Think of beige; if there is more of one primary than the other two in the starting brown, the resulting beige will take on a yellow, red, or blue tint. This is most obvious when looking at the beige next to each of the three primary colors. That explains why all your khaki pants are not the same color. It also explains why it is so hard to find fabrics to use as skin tones—some are too yellow, some too red, and others too blue.

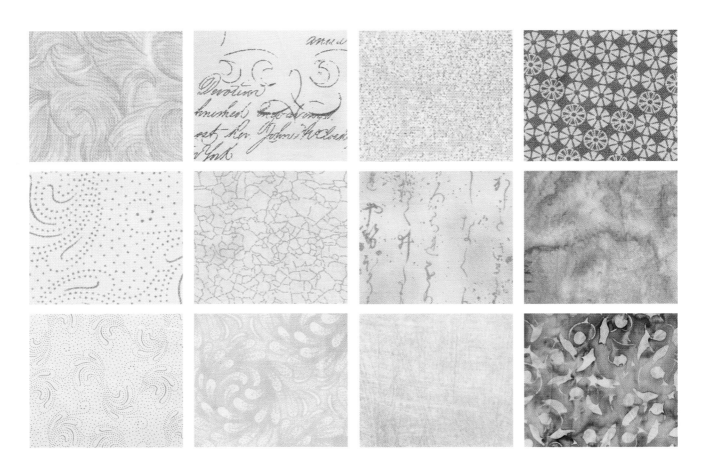

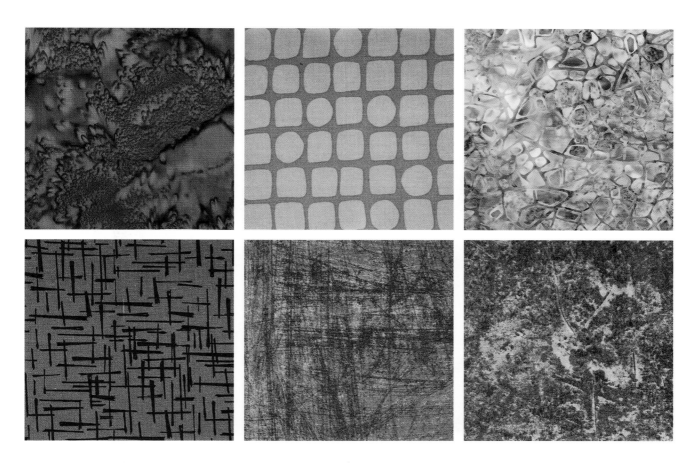

Believe it or not, not all black fabrics are pure black, either, which means grays can also have an underlying color tone to them. Often, fabrics viewed alone will look like true gray, but when put with another fabric, one might look very blue (or pink or yellow, and so on). This also explains why not all black fabrics "match" when used together.

When you mix beige and gray together in equal amounts, the resulting color is taupe. Now that you know that the path to each part of the recipe was fraught with pitfalls, you can understand why taupes can also be warm or cool, with undertones of yellow, blue, or red. One of the most frustrating aspects of working with commercial fabric is finding grays, beiges, and taupes that work well together and possess the color temperature you need.

Looking for their complementary colors? Gray, beige, brown, and taupe do not have complements, nor do they have analogous colors because they are true neutrals. Their temperature is set only when one of the primaries dominates the recipe.

Moving Away from Realistic Color

When you translate a photo into fabric, you do not need to reproduce the colors as shown in the original. You can make changes that are subtle, to establish a focal point, or you can completely change the colors. Remember, this is your artwork, and staying true to the realistic colors does not have to be a part of making art.

Let's imagine a landscape photo taken in the fall. You love the landscape, but you want to create a winter scene. Just change the color—white in place of green and cooler tones instead of oranges and reds. As long as the values are correct, the color doesn't have to be.

Landscape, Summer

Landscape,
Winter

Landscape,
Fall

Want to go really crazy? No problem. Stay true to the value in the pattern and remember your color principles—you are ready to create a masterpiece.

Jagged

If you plan to move away from realistic color, it may be easier to print your pattern in black and white rather than in full color. This means you can see the changes in values without being distracted by the actual color in the photo. I always find that it helps to have the color photo available for reference, just in case it becomes hard to tell where one gray area ends and another begins.

By understanding and learning to use color, you will be better able to control the mood you set, the distance you create in your composition, and even where you want to focus the attention of a viewer. These rules apply whether your quilts are representational or abstract. Look at art by others, and really focus on the way colors are used—the saturation, the values, and the colors themselves. By paying attention to the way other artists make use of color, you will develop a set of criteria to think about when choosing color for your future artworks.

THE TRUE VALUE OF UNDERSTANDING VALUE

What Is Value?

Value can be as important as, or even more important than, color alone. No matter how sophisticated your understanding of the use of color, your results will suffer if you don't apply the simple rules of value.

Value is not hard to understand—light, medium, dark. That is it. If you came from the world of traditional quilting, you know that mantra—*every quilt benefits from light, medium, and dark fabrics in combination*. So does all art.

Think about a black-and-white photograph—no color, just black, white, and shades of gray. No matter how many shades of gray are present in the photo, it will appear flat and uninteresting unless black and white are present. Why? Contrast. The lightness of the white and the darkness of the black, combined with a range of grays in between, make the photograph come alive. Even without color, the brain reads and understands a black-and-white photo as reality when all the values are in the right place. We aren't bothered by gray faces; if the values are correct, the brain makes the jump.

Now think about art quilts—or any artwork—the same way. If the colors you choose include a variety of light, medium, and dark tones, the quilt will have contrast and will look lively and exciting. Leave out the light and dark (the black and white of our photo example) and the remainder of the colors (all the gray tones) will blend together.

When the values of the fabrics are too close, the whole composition blends together in *Self-Portrait 1*.

When values are distinctly different, the result is more dramatic in *Self-Portrait 2*.

This is also true of artwork that contains only light tones or only dark ones. No contrast means no visual excitement. And, like a black-and-white photo, the colors do not need to be true to life. That is great news, because it means there are a lot of options to have fun and go wild with color. You do not need to be a slave to the original colors in your starting photo. Do you want to create a face in all blue tones? Just stay true to the values in the pattern and use blues instead of beiges. How about a yellow tree or a purple cow? If the values are correct, the results will work. Your brain will accept it, just as it accepts the black-and-white photo—because all the contours, the dimension, and the shadows are present, expressed by the correct changes in value.

Old Woman

Value is relative—meaning a fabric that may be light in one quilt could actually be the dark value in another. We need to think about light, medium, and dark as they relate to each other in combination. Most of us, when building a stash of fabrics, tend to collect fabrics whose values fall in the same range—usually sort of medium values. It is important to include lighter fabrics and darker fabrics to round out your assortment. When building a stash from which to work, buying a range of values means you will have the right options when you need them.

Purple fabrics in a variety of values

How to Determine Value

Often, the differences in the values of fabrics can be seen with the naked eye. Sometimes they can be seen by squinting. For most fabric selection (and to avoid wrinkles around your eyes), you can see the differences in value by using a red viewer (like a Ruby Beholder or a piece of red photo gel). This is just a small piece of red plastic—nothing exotic about it—that is held about 6″ from your eye, through which your fabrics are viewed. The red cancels out the colors, leaving only their values (for red or orange fabrics, you need to use a green viewer because all reds or all oranges will look alike through the red one). Like taking a black-and-white photo of the potential fabrics, looking through a red viewer will instantly tell you if there are light, medium, and dark values, as well as how they relate to each other, and you won't be confused or distracted by the actual colors.

Just knowing the difference, however, doesn't necessarily help you find the right value when choosing fabric. This is why I designed a card I call the Art Quilter's Value Scale (page 117). Nothing fancy or exotic, it shows gradations of gray, from white to black, along the edges. Each gray value is numbered. All you need to do is look at the Value Scale next to your pattern, slide it along until you can establish which gray is the closest in value to that area, and assign the corresponding number. Then, you take the Value Scale to your potential fabrics and find one with the same value number.

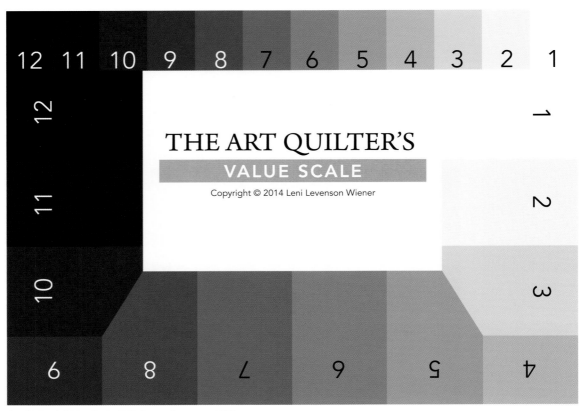

Art Quilter's Value Scale (full-size card on page 117)

Zingers

Fabrics aren't always a single color or value, however, and that might seem as if it will complicate the process. Look at a single printed fabric and you will see that it usually "reads" like a light, medium, or dark as it relates to your other fabrics—and that is how they are assigned. Sometimes you will encounter fabrics that look like they can move around in the assortment, with so many colors or values in them that they defy pinning down. I call these *zingers*. A zinger can be hard to fit neatly into a particular value—but that is fine. A few zingers here and there add visual excitement to your work, so don't avoid them just because where they fit isn't obvious at first glance. Usually, a zinger is used in an area that is relatively small, so it does not distract attention as it might in a larger area.

Print Density and Value

The density of the print will also affect how its value reads. A print that is small and spread out will read more like the value of its background; while those with tight, close patterns may read differently. Large-scale prints present their own set of options; using a certain part of that large-scale print might be just the right thing in a particular spot—even if the rest of the print is not even close. Fussy cutting (which means to cut a very specific part of the fabric) just one part of the print means that only the value of that cut piece is relevant.

Changes in Value

The number of fabrics you use in a particular area of your work will determine the difference required in value variations from one to the next. Take a face, for example. If the face is made up of eleven different fabrics, the difference in value from one fabric to the next can be subtle, giving a beautiful blending effect to the face. But, if you are using only four fabrics on that same face, the change in values must be more pronounced to make the jump from the lightest to the darkest in fewer increments. These are decisions you will make as you create your pattern, and the values will be laid out for you. Then choosing fabric is as easy as matching the values on the pattern to the fabrics in your stash.

Here is a little secret not everyone will admit—I don't always get it right the first time. Sometimes, while working on an art quilt, something just doesn't seem right. More often than not, it is value. When I try another fabric with the correct value in place of the one that isn't working, the whole design starts to come together. Occasionally, I need to do this more than once. It is amazing how changing a single fabric can turn a problem quilt into something wonderful.

Detail of *Old Man* (full quilt on page 92)

Examples of faces using multiple fabrics

Old Woman

Detail of *After* (full quilt on page 42)

Detail of *In the Moment* (full quilt on page 41)

Examples of faces using only a few fabrics

Value and Color Complements

Using complementary colors will bring life and excitement to a quilt, but it does not mean you must use them in the same values. They will be more interesting and effective if you vary the values of the complementary colors. Think about red and green Christmas colors—the use of red and green in the same value. The impact is strong and in-your-face. Now, think about green leaves with a pink flower—the same green but a red in a different *value*, which changes the dynamics. The complement still does its job, but varying the value can soften the punch.

It isn't an accident that high school football teams and commercial advertising make use of complementary colors together in similar values. They seem to vibrate, and therefore attract attention. A quilt that utilizes color and value this way will also have a visual jolt. But changing one of the values of the two complementary colors makes them easier on the eye, reducing the shocking effect while also retaining the visual excitement. All determined by controlling the value—pretty remarkable.

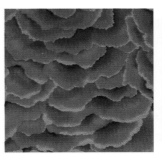

Red and green of similar values

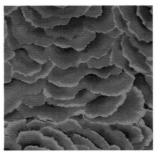

Red and green in varied values

PATTERN AND PRINT SCALE

Small-, Medium-, and Large-Scale Prints

Often overlooked in discussions of fabric selection is print scale. Any fabric that is not a solid color contains a small-, medium-, or large-scale pattern. Like value, scale is relative—what may be a small-scale print in one fabric assortment could be medium scale in another. Density also affects the way print scale appears; some prints are closely packed, while others have a lot of background showing through.

Just as variations in value and color will make a quilt more dynamic, variations in scale will, too. So, it is important to use small-, medium-, and large-scale prints in combination to create layers of complexity that make the overall quilt look more interesting and nuanced. If all the prints are similar in scale, the results will look choppy and confusing.

A print with curved or swirling shapes will add movement to the look of the finished quilt. One that is small and static will make the quilt appear more sedate and calm. The choice of print, like the choice of color, will contribute a lot to the mood of the finished piece.

Size Matters

In recent years more large-scale prints have been appearing in quilt shops. These offer their own distinct pros and cons and, for art quilts, must be treated differently than fabrics with small- or medium-scale prints.

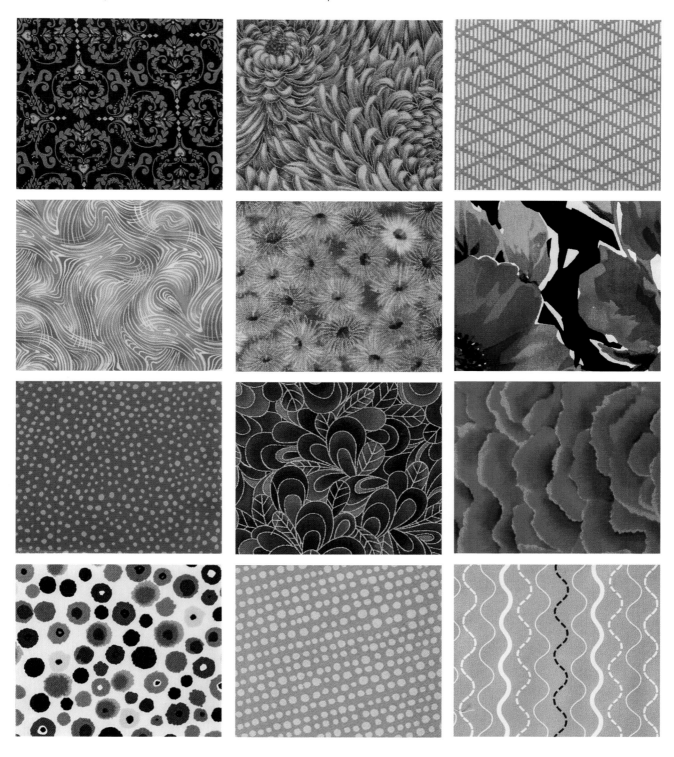

When considering print scale, the size of your finished quilt is key. Imagine a fabric with a fairly large-scale print in a quilt that measures 14" square. After cutting into it, you won't see most of the print anymore. The opportunity for fussy cutting is particularly useful in giving you several different looks from one large-scale print fabric. Small areas can serve an entirely different function in the quilt than they did in the fabric—like a flower petal with subtle shading in the fabric print that works perfectly as human lips.

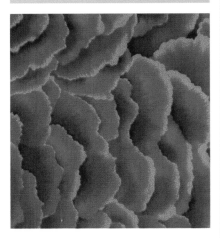

Now imagine the same large-scale print in a quilt that is 60" square. There, the entire print could show, and the pattern and its repeat will have significant impact on the overall look of the finished quilt.

The smaller the finished quilt, the more focus should be placed on using small- to medium-scale prints. Larger quilts will allow for larger-scale prints.

The Unexpected

Personally, I like to use a wide variety of commercially available prints in my art quilts, particularly when the pattern seems unusual or unexpected. That little surprise, the added drama and the nod to fabric as the material (literally) from which the art quilt is made, makes the work more intriguing—and has become a hallmark of my art quilts.

Fabrics used in *Pears* might seem unlikely.

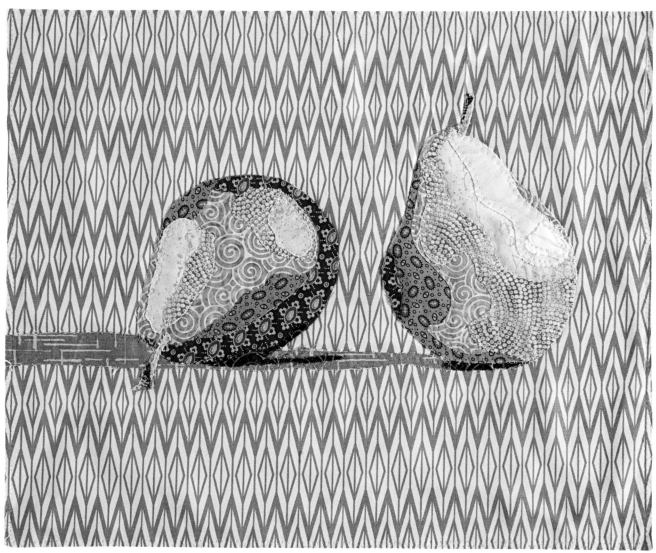

Pears

I try to avoid the obvious—a print that looks like rocks, for instance, used in the stone wall of a building. The scale of the rocks or their perspective may not be exactly the right fit, but more than that it looks too studied. I prefer to find an interesting and unexpected print or batik that gives the illusion of rocks without being so literal. The same is true for prints with grass or flowers, bricks or basket weave. Finding a fabric that will "read" like the texture you want to depict (especially when it is unexpected) is more artful and compelling. Look at these art quilts and the fabrics from which they are made. Some of the choices might surprise you.

Fabrics used in the face of *Old Man* may surprise you (full quilt on page 92).

A black-and-white floral may not be the first thing you think of when looking at a tree. Detail of *Iola Birches* (full quilt on page 80).

The multiple unexpected fabrics used in this girl's hair have different print scales. Detail of *Multifabric Hair* (full quilt on page 103).

Fabrics used in girl's hair

When building your stash of fabrics, it is important to remember that a fabric print that serves only one limited function will not be as useful in your stash as one that can be used in many different ways. Instead, collect fabrics that can be used in a wide variety of applications. I call these my "universal donors." Looking through this book you will find the same fabrics used over and over to depict entirely different textures. For me, this is part of the fun of using fabric as my basic building block when making art quilts.

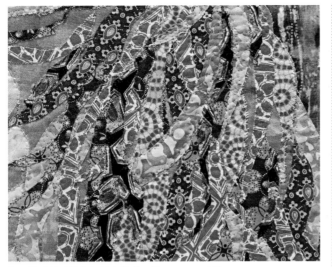

Detail of *Multifabric Hair* (full quilt on page 103)

Landscape, Fall

Detail of *Pears* (full quilt on page 31)

Parrot

The same fabric is used for hair and the dark shadow of the pear.

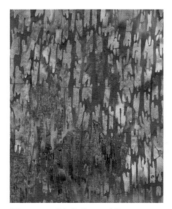

The same fabric is used for water and feathers.

Solids, Batiks, and Hand-Dyes

Some quilters do not like working with prints at all. Of course, you can work with solid-color fabrics, if you prefer. Many quilters who use only solid-color fabrics dye their own in order to have subtle value variations of each color—since solids are not as plentiful in quilt shops as prints. And remember, you will need a greater variety of solid fabrics to depict light and shadow than you would need if you used that perfect print or batik that has more than one value in it and you fussy cut it to do the job.

Batiks are a nice balance between solid-colored fabrics and more exuberant prints. They are often a single color with lighter and darker areas that give the illusion of texture or shadow. Batiks can also combine subtly blended colors that can be used in an area that called for more than a single fabric, beautifully representing things like rocks, trees, water, or sky.

Like batiks, hand-dyed fabrics have variations of value and color and can look like works of art all by themselves. These can be expensive, so when I buy them, I save them for backgrounds and places where the fabric will really stand out. There are many commercial *hand-dyed look-alikes* available now that have the same wonderful advantages as hand-dyes, at a more reasonable cost.

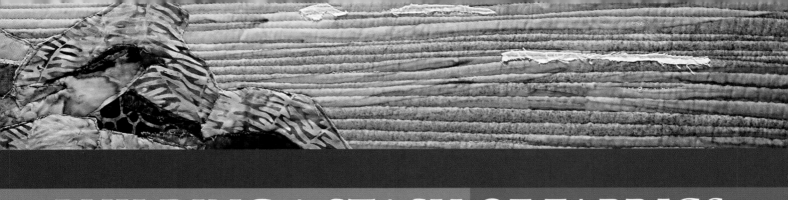

BUILDING A STASH OF FABRICS

Your fabrics are your art supplies, and having an assortment of choices available makes your work easier and as a result, more pleasurable. You will want to audition different options before making final decisions. Having to go to the fabric store every time you want to try a new possibility becomes cumbersome and unworkable.

Your fabric stash is your palette and must provide you with all sorts of possibilities, not just colors and prints you like. Each fabric used will support the artwork as only one small component. Never was the old expression "Use what the quilt wants, not what you want" more meaningful than it is for art quilt fabrics.

What to Look For

For this process, you will need to change the way you think about fabric. You will be looking for fabrics with perceived textures and movement rather than beautiful prints. Focus on *tone-on-tone* fabrics that appear to have both light and dark values of a single color rather than on a print that makes its own strong statement. Geometrics, swirls, dots, and other monochromatic small- to medium-scale prints will probably make up most of your stash. Batiks and hand-dyes (either handmade or commercially printed) are beautiful blenders and backgrounds. Don't get hung up on collecting only one kind of fabric; the combination of all these kinds of fabrics is what transforms a photo into a work of fabric art.

Try to avoid fabrics with their own agenda, like strong patterns, fabrics with specific pictures on them, or those that might have limited use in a variety of quilt designs. Keep in mind that novelty prints or those resembling rock, brick, or wood grain may not be the right scale or perspective for your quilt, and therefore those textures are better being "built" from other fabrics in your stash—and this looks more artistic, as well.

Since I prefer to work on small quilts, large-scale patterns have only a small place in my stash. I usually fussy cut, so a particular area of a larger design serves a completely different purpose in my artwork than it did in the original fabric print. Unless you make

large quilts, multicolored patterns or large-scale prints may be something you never buy and most likely will have a limited role in the assortment needed to complete your work.

First and foremost, you must know yourself and your artistic style. An art quilter who works with representational images will require a greater range of colors and patterns than an art quilter whose work is abstract. For representational art quilts, you must have at your disposal a collection of fabrics that will work as stone, bark, grass, skin, feathers, fur, and a wide array of other perceived textures. Surprisingly, however, the same fabrics can be used to illustrate many of these textures and ideas. Representational art quilts have areas of light and shadow, so it is necessary to collect a range of values from very light fabrics to dark browns, grays, and black, even if they are not your favorite colors. If you plan to do nature studies or landscapes, collect more browns and greens (in shades from almost white to almost black); if you do faces, skin tones and hair require that you collect more beige and brown fabrics.

Stripes are another consideration. If you prefer landscapes or seascapes, straight-line stripes may be too severe for the kind of art quilts you make. Instead, look for stripes with curving and irregular lines, which will appear more organic. However, if you are depicting still water or buildings, room interiors, and other man-made elements in your art quilts, the straight and even stripe may be your friend.

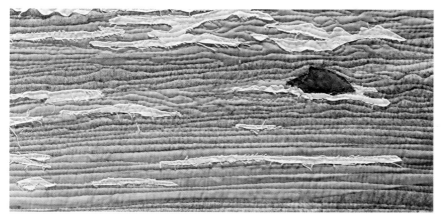

Curvy-line striped fabric. Detail of *Shifting Tide* (full quilt on page 85).

Straight-line striped fabric. Detail of *Purple Seascape* (full quilt on page 86).

The print scale will vary depending on the size of the pieces you tend to produce. Most art quilters have an approximate size they are most comfortable making. Obviously if your works are large, you should have more larger-scale prints; but if small, these will be less important to you, and your stash should reflect that.

Don't shy away from some fabrics with personality; these will be used sparingly as zingers in your art quilts. These might include African or Asian prints or those with strong multicolored patterns that can be used to add a little spice to your art quilt.

Organizing Your Palette

By storing my fabrics by color (I use separate large plastic stacking bins designed for under-bed storage), I can find what I want easily. I can instantly see where I may have gaps, so I know what colors to focus on when I find myself in a quilt shop. My personal preference is for orange, blue, and green. I collect a small amount of purple, pink, and yellow (not favorites of mine) because I understand their importance in certain places, and a surprisingly large amount of brown, gray, white, and black. Because I make a lot of quilts of people, I buy every "clean" beige fabric I find (page 16). I do not purchase with a particular quilt in mind, preferring to collect general categories—fabrics that may be good for water, sky, trees, skin, or hair—or those very exciting fabrics that could work in so many areas that they become my "universal donors." I have a personal fondness for fabrics with writing on them and for interesting black-and-white prints, so I purchase larger cuts of these when I find them.

  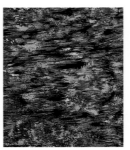  

Whatever your favorite color is (the color you find yourself using most in your quilts), collect some of its complement. For example, if you love green, collect some pinks and reds as well. Using a complementary color will make your quilt more visually exciting, so you want to have those options on hand. Remember to buy different values of every color—light, medium, and dark fabrics will serve you well whenever you need to find the right match.

How Much to Purchase

Knowing how much to purchase is a function of the quilt size you are comfortable making. Some artists work small, while others prefer to make large quilts. If you regularly make quilts that are five feet square, for example, you will need larger cuts of each fabric (especially for backgrounds) than for journal quilts that are only one foot square. Understanding your own preferences is the best key to knowing what and how much to collect.

Most of my quilts are fairly small, so my general rule of thumb is to purchase only a quarter yard (or fat quarters, if they are available) of each fabric, allowing an expansion of my fabric stash for a relatively modest financial investment. I will purchase half a yard if a fabric seems like a universal donor—if I can see it working in a wider range of situations. In rare

cases, I will purchase a yard or more if I think the fabric will make a great background, for fabrics I know I will use a lot, or for those that will require a larger single piece of fabric—usually as part of the background—like water, sky, grass, or sand.

You do not need to limit yourself to cotton. You can include fabrics with actual texture, not just perceived texture. Shop in the home-decor department or the garment-fabric department of your favorite fabric stores, or go to the Salvation Army or other resale stores to look for old clothes you can cut up. In my house, no garment is given away or thrown away before I get first crack at it as a fabric source. Even garments with stains or holes can be great candidates. Silk neckties, with their gorgeous patterns, are a bit tricky to work with but can be great options.

When to Buy the Whole Bolt

Finally, think about purchasing a bolt of whatever fabric you like to use for your quilt backs. Since art quilts hang on the wall, don't use a beautiful print that will never be seen—unless, of course, that is part of your individual style. I use good-quality muslin or cotton canvas for the backs of all my art quilts—it gives my work continuity. I purchase a fifteen-yard bolt (often on sale), which lasts a long time. That way, I never need to worry about whether or not I have enough fabric for the back of my quilt, and I don't have to use up a print that might have been just what I needed down the road.

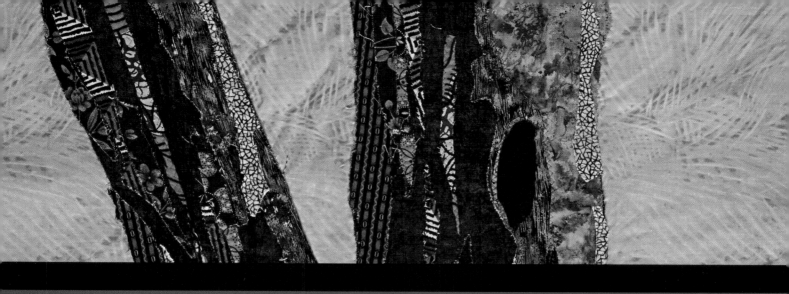

SECTION TWO
MAKING AN ART QUILT
STEP BY STEP

GETTING STARTED

In this section, we will make an art quilt together, step by step. The sample project I have chosen is from a photo I took several years ago. I chose to use it here for several reasons: It has a tree and a natural setting as the background and two figures whose faces do not need a lot of detail, so it is not too intimidating as a starting point. Even if you don't adore this photo, you will learn a lot by working through it with me.

This section begins with a description of how to create and print a pattern from a photo of your choice. However, for the sample project, I have provided the pattern for you, including my pencil guidelines and value markings. You can either scan it or take a digital photo of it, and then print it in any size you wish. Then follow along with me as I walk you through the steps to transform it into an art quilt. When you understand the process, you will know how to make an art quilt from any photo.

Explorers (project on page 47)

Choosing a Photo

The photo you choose as your starting point is very important for a successful quilt. Look for photos that tell an intriguing story, and crop in close to eliminate any extraneous background that does not support the subject of your art quilt. The stronger the image, the more successful the art quilt will be.

It is important to remember that permission is required before you can exhibit or publish any works you make from photos that are not your own (including from the patterns in this book). For your own use, you can make an art quilt from any photo you find. If the photo is not yours, you need to ask permission from the photographer before you make your art quilt public or sell it.

Choosing the Size of Your Art Quilt

There are several things to consider when deciding on the final size of your quilt. How much space do you have to do your work? How much time do you want to spend making your quilt? How fussy do you want to get with a lot of little pieces for details? For a variety of reasons, most quilters find a comfort zone in which they like to work.

I like to make rather small art quilts, usually smaller than 20" on any side. I can finish them quickly and move on to another image. I don't need large pieces of fabric in my stash, and I can work from all the little scraps I can't bring myself to throw away. Finally, and for me most significantly, functional stitch lines (see Functional Sewing, page 74) in some of the larger areas of fabric detract from the more graphic look I want in my art quilts. Keeping the quilts small reduces the need for functional quilting. You can decide on the quilt size that makes the most sense for you.

Preparing Your Image

In the next section you will be given instructions to make your pattern on the computer using photo-editing software. I use either GIMP (a free program), Adobe Photoshop, or Adobe Photoshop Elements (see page 43). When making your pattern, you decide the level of detail you wish to convey in your quilt.

In the Moment

Catnap is very detailed, which meant using a lot of little pieces of fabric.

Neither level of detail is right and neither is wrong—it is up to you as the artist. When you bring your image into the computer program of your choice, play with it and decide whether you want a lot of detail or not as much.

The central figure in *After* has much less detail and therefore required fewer pieces of fabric.

Making and Printing a Pattern from Your Photo

For many years, I have instructed students to use Adobe Photoshop or Photoshop Elements to make "patterns" from their photos. Photoshop has a filter called Cutout, which reduces the number of visible colors, resulting in what looks like a paint-by-number pattern that is easy to follow when choosing and cutting fabric. When preparing a pattern using the Photoshop Cutout filter, you can go to a maximum of only eight "levels," which essentially means reducing the image to eight colors. This often necessitates applying the Cutout filter in small sections at a time, which some people find confusing. The resulting pattern does have nice, clear demarcations between the color changes and is a good way to prepare a pattern if you are comfortable using the program.

Some of my students have found Adobe Photoshop and Photoshop Elements complicated to learn and others do not want to purchase a program, so now I recommend GIMP, a free download that is simpler to use for our purposes. GIMP has a sliding scale that allows you to see how the pattern will look. The divisions between colors are not as hard-edged as in Photoshop, but the distinction is clear enough to use as a guide while making your quilt. I use GIMP all the time now.

If you do not want to make your own pattern, please visit my website at www.leniwiener.com for information about how to purchase a custom pattern from your photo that will be emailed to you.

Using GIMP

When I begin making a pattern from a digital photo, I save a copy of the photo on my computer's desktop to work from. That way I can find it easily, but even more importantly, I preserve the original digital file untouched. (Never save an alteration to an original photo file; instead, always save your changes with a different name so that the original file remains unaltered.)

Go to www.gimp.org and follow the instructions to download GIMP—it is free. I keep the icon right on my desktop, so it is easy to find and use when I need it.

Installing GIMP for Mac users

Mac OS X users should be able to download GIMP according to the instructions provided.

For other Mac operating systems, you need to do an additional step: When you go to the Download page, look for Macports and click Download Macports. Proceed to click Download on the top right corner of the Macports page.

After Macports is installed, the installation of GIMP should proceed as described for PCs.

Open GIMP and you will see a blank white screen with tools across the top and down the left side. To bring your photo into the program, select File (top left corner) and then Open. A screen will then open with a list of options. On the left, select Desktop (or the location where you saved the file on your computer), and search for and select your photo. In the right-hand column, you may see a preview of the photo; if not, you can click the question mark to preview the image and make sure it is the photo you wanted.

When you find the photo, click Open (bottom right corner) and the photo will appear on the screen. Note: You may first see a window that asks if you want the program to *convert* the image. This means your photo is in a color format that the program can't read. Don't worry—just click the Convert tab and your photo will appear.

Now you have the photo on the screen. It is not necessary to change your photo now, but if you want to lighten it (which is sometimes helpful if the photo is dark), pull down the Colors menu at the top. Select Brightness-Contrast, and then use the sliding scale to adjust the brightness or the contrast or both. When the photo looks the way you want, click OK.

Pull down the Colors menu, and then select Posterize. This will instantly reduce the image to only a few colors. Using the slide labeled Posterize Levels, slide slowly from 3 up until you find a number that shows a pattern you can follow. These changes will show on the screen as you go, so there is no need to guess (if you do not see the changes on the screen, make sure the Preview checkbox is selected). I find that somewhere between 5 and 11 will produce patterns that are easy to follow, but every picture is different and every person can fine-tune the pattern to the desired level of detail. While evaluating, concentrate primarily on the main elements of the photo (solid-color backgrounds may start to look like a lot of color blotches, but this is not important; the more important consideration is that the main elements in the photo look like a level of detail that you will find manageable). Personally, I like the patterns to be simple, requiring fewer pieces of fabric and sacrificing fine detail for a more graphic-art look. But you decide how much detail you want in your art quilt, and stop sliding the Posterize scale accordingly.

When you find the number that looks like a good pattern, click OK. Let's say, for example, you chose Posterize Level 5. Now pull down the File menu, scroll down to and select Export, and the file name will appear in the top box. Be sure to change the file name to read something like *"original photo name_gimp5"* as a reference, and then double-click the Export button at the bottom of the screen. A window will appear with a sliding scale for quality; make sure the slider is at 75% or higher, and click Export (in the bottom middle) to close this box.

Now your new working pattern and your old photo should appear on your desktop (or wherever you saved the original file). If you click the red X in the top right corner of the GIMP screen, it will close this particular photo image. It will first ask if you want to change the original photo; select the center option Close Without Saving (you have already saved it with another name). Now you can open another photo, or click the red X in the top right corner again to close the program completely.

While you are working, remember that there is a History column on the right side of your screen that will allow you to go back one or more steps if you run into difficulty. You can also use the Undo button by pulling down the Edit menu and selecting Undo. If you feel you have gone totally haywire, simply close the program and, when asked if you want to save changes, click No. Then you can start again.

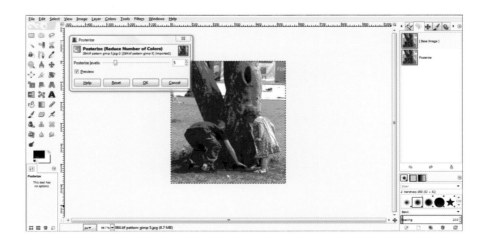

Printing Your Full-Size Pattern

After you have made your pattern, you need to print it the actual size of your finished art quilt to use as your guide in cutting and placing fabric pieces.

I recommend www.blockposters.com, a web-based program that sizes your image. This website requires no registration, does not cost anything, and is easy to use. You do not even need to download anything; everything is done online.

I always print both the pattern and the original photo in the same size so that I can compare them while working. This helps with fine details that may have been lost in the pattern; and since the pattern usually shifts a bit in color, having the original on hand in the same size can be helpful.

Blockposters.com will not work on a photo larger than 1 MB. To find out how large a file your picture is, right click on it and select Properties. In this box, you will see Size with the file size of your pattern. If it is larger than 1 MB, you must resize it. Most photo programs will allow you to resize photographs—often just by selecting the percentage to reduce. Check the Help files to see how to do this for your particular photo program.

Open your Internet browser and go to blockposters.com. About halfway down the page, select Click Here to Start. This opens a page that says Upload Your Picture. Click the white Browse button.

Select the location on your computer where you saved your file. (If you saved the pattern and original photo on your desktop, it is easy to find.) At this point the picture does not appear on the screen—don't be alarmed—but you should see the file name. Now click the Continue button (written in red at the lower right corner of the screen).

Your picture will appear with a window to the right of it. (If this does not occur, chances are your photo was more than 1 MB. Resize it and try again.) In this box you will choose several options:

How many pages wide? Click the right and left arrows to tell the program how many pages **wide** you want your art quilt pattern to be. If you are printing in portrait (vertical) orientation, each page is about 8″ wide. If you are printing in landscape (horizontal) orientation, each page is about 10.5″ wide.

Choose either Portrait or Landscape orientation (if your photo is horizontal, it is usually best to use Landscape; if your photo is vertical, it is best to use Portrait) by selecting the appropriate circle.

The default paper size is set at A4; you will need to select the circle next to Letter US for standard U.S. printer paper size.

At the bottom of this window, the program will tell you the approximate size of your finished poster (in your case, your art quilt pattern).

Click Continue.

You will now see a message in red that says, *Congratulations, your poster has been created. Click here to download a PDF file containing your images.* Your picture will not be visible on the screen. Click the message, and a PDF file containing all the pages of your pattern will appear. From here you can print the file and/or save it. I save it by selecting the File menu, then Save Page As, and then save it to the desktop. I recommend saving the PDF so you can reference it later or reprint it, if necessary.

Often the pattern will not be as clear in some areas, and the colors will probably have changed a bit, so having the full-size photo available is helpful. Therefore, I recommend that you prepare the original photo in the same size and orientation you used for the pattern and print them both.

Now your pattern is printed in the actual size your art quilt will be and ready to put together. Line up the pages in order, trim off the small white border on one sheet so you can overlap the pages, and tape them together. This will give you a pattern in the full finished size of your art quilt, and you can also print a full-size copy of the original photo if you want.

I find it helpful to begin with a mechanical pencil and draw along the edges of the color changes. If you created your pattern in Photoshop, these lines will be more obvious than if you used GIMP; but either way you can see the changes in value and/or color. Trace around these changes on the pattern, simplifying any little jig-jags in the edges and making them clearer to follow when tracing onto freezer paper. We will talk more about this as we start on our project.

ART QUILT PROCESS AT A GLANCE

1. Make the pattern using GIMP, Photoshop, or Photoshop Elements.

2. Print a full-size pattern and the original photo using www.blockposters.com; then tape it together.

3. Trace the edges of the pattern along the color changes.

4. Establish and mark the value numbers using Art Quilter's Value Scale.

5. Start with one element.

6. Choose fabrics.

7. Determine the layering.

8. Use a lightbox or window to trace the sections of the element onto freezer paper.

9. Press freezer paper onto the fabric and cut out pieces.

10. Put fabric pieces in place and keep going. Use tracing-paper template where necessary.

11. Step back and evaluate.

12. Glue each element together as it is completed.

13. Build all additional elements.

14. Decide on the background.

15. Glue everything together.

16. Sew the pieces in place with or without batting.

17. Add the back.

18. Finish the edges.

EXPLORERS PROJECT

Original photo

Photo by author

Image cropped and pattern prepared using GIMP

Image cropped and pattern prepared using Adobe Photoshop
(or Photoshop Elements)

Finished *Explorers* quilt

I have already prepared the pattern for this project using GIMP (page 43), so all you need to do is photocopy the pattern sheets (pages 120–123) and enlarge or reduce the size, if desired. I recommend printing the pattern the size it appears in the book, which is two pieces of paper wide in both directions (four pieces: two for the top and two for the bottom). However, you can make this quilt any size you want; the steps do not change. I recommend this size because the pieces will be manageable but the overall art quilt will not be so large that it becomes overwhelming.

Print your pattern pages and tape them together by trimming the white border off the side of one page and overlapping it on the white border of the adjoining page. I have already drawn the guidelines and value numbers for you.

I keep the photo handy, either printed or on my iPad or laptop, so I can refer to it whenever some of the little details are lost in the pattern. It also gives me a more accurate rendition of the original colors, since the pattern-making process may have shifted or even eliminated colors. For this project, you may refer to the original photo (page 47).

Breaking Your Composition into Elements

Original GIMP pattern in full color

Pattern in lighter color with traced edges and value numbers

To easily explain my process, I traced the edges and marked the correct values on the full-size pattern (pages 120–123). The pattern appears much lighter than the original GIMP image so that you can see the marked pencil lines and value numbers. Since the full-size pattern is deliberately lighter, the assigned value numbers will not appear to be correct. Use the full-color and unmarked pattern (page 48) to practice finding the values numbers.

The quilt is built in steps by breaking the composition into manageable bites that I call *elements*. Working on the elements one at a time is less intimidating and gives you a logical place to start and an easy way to progress. After the pattern is broken into elements, each element is addressed separately, in whichever order you think makes sense.

In our project, the elements are the boy, the girl, the tree, and the background. We will begin with the girl, since the figures are the focal point of the composition. Then, we will complete the boy, the tree, and finally the environment in which they will be placed.

For now, look only at the girl in the pattern; everything else in the composition is irrelevant.

The Girl

BREAKING ELEMENTS INTO SECTIONS

Each element is divided into *sections*. Here the girl is made up of four different sections—her skin (face, arms, and legs), her dress, her hair, and her sandals. When we look at values to choose fabrics for the girl, we will be looking at one section at a time.

ESTABLISHING VALUES IN THE PATTERN

Establishing the value changes in the pattern makes it easier to choose appropriate fabrics. To determine the values, I have developed the Art Quilter's Value Scale (page 117). This scale shows values from white to black with 10 shades of gray in between. Each of these 12 values has a number assigned, which I call the value numbers. These will allow you to see the progression from one value to the next and match fabric values to those in the pattern. Cut out the Art Quilter's Value Scale printed in the book and glue it to a piece of cardboard. (If you prefer, you can purchase one from www.leniwiener.com.)

NOTE

If you either photocopy or scan and print the Art Quilter's Value Scale (page 117) from the book, the gray values may not be exactly the same as shown in the book. This will not make a big a difference since the card allows you to match the value in the pattern with the value of the fabric. Just be sure you use the same printed card when establishing the pattern and fabric values for a given project; consistency is what matters.

Let's start with the dress, as it is the largest part of the figure. This dress is four different values: a light, medium, and dark value and just a hint of an even darker value at the bottom of her skirt hem and top of her arm. I have already drawn the guidelines on the pattern and identified their values, but go through these steps with me so you will understand how to do it when you work on your own photos and patterns.

1 Using the side of the card with all 12 values in a row, slide the edge of the card along next to the middle value of the dress until you find the gray that most resembles the value in the pattern.

2 Note the corresponding value number directly onto your pattern.

You can use the larger squares on the other three sides of the card to confirm your decision if you are not sure. I see it as either a 3 or a 4, and that will depend on the fabrics I have on hand and what I think would look good here. The next value in the dress is the darker value; here I am calling it a 6. The lightest part of the dress looks like a 1 or a 2. The little bit of the underside of the skirt hem is the final value—8. If you have difficulty determining the value, make an educated guess. If it falls between two numbers, say 7 and 8, call it 7½. If you really have trouble identifying the values, you can print your pattern in black and white (most printers will allow you to print using only black ink in the Properties window). But remember you are finding relationships between values, which is more important than a specific number, so don't make yourself crazy.

Establish values in pattern.

Write value numbers on pattern.

Now you can begin the most creative part of the process, choosing fabrics.

CHOOSING FABRICS

Your first decision is whether you intend to stay true to the colors in the original photo or go in a different direction. It doesn't matter which you choose—the process is the same.

If you want the girl in a different-colored dress rather than pink, go for it. I think the pink is a nice complement to the green grass.

Since I organize my fabric stash by color, it is easy for me to find the bin containing all my pink fabrics.

1 Choose several fabrics you think might work—more options than you will ultimately use—so you can look at different fabrics as they relate to the values in the pattern and each other. Use the larger squares on the Value Scale to find fabrics with the same value number you established in the pattern.

Think about having a variety of print scales, and maybe even one or two zingers (see Zingers, page 25) that will enliven your element. Consider the backs of fabrics and fussy cutting areas of a fabric that may be different in color or value from the rest of the print.

Compare fabric with Value Scale.

2 Match the values of the pattern to the values of the fabrics to narrow down your fabrics to an assortment of four fabrics you like together. Remember: This is an art, not a science; so nuance is allowed.

 NOTE

Some teachers and books recommend making a black-and-white photocopy of your potential fabrics so you can see their values. I do not find this helpful, because subtleties in value are not clear enough to see this way. Although some values are obvious to the naked eye, the Art Quilter's Value Scale is the easiest and most accurate way to determine those subtle changes.

3 If you are working with three or more fabrics, make a quick guide by taping snippets of the fabrics you have chosen to a piece of paper with the value number written next to each one. This is just a guide in case you get confused—any way you choose to keep track is fine.

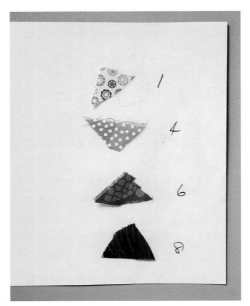

Fabric guide for the girl's dress

4 Put away the fabric you won't be using in your quilt. Removing the other options you considered from your work surface will help you stay organized and will also give you more room to work.

CUTTING THE PIECES

Now you need to decide in what order to cut your fabric. If you were to cut each piece of fabric exactly as the pattern indicates and try to butt them up against each other, there would be inevitable movement when you sew them, resulting in gaps. You also want every element to be self-contained, so it must be built on a foundation with the other fabrics overlapping.

Usually the foundation or base fabric is the one that occupies the largest area in the section, but sometimes when you are working from smaller pieces, you won't have enough of a single fabric to use as the foundation. So choose one of the other fabrics in the assortment. It doesn't really matter. I used the value 6 fabric as the foundation.

Freezer Paper

Freezer paper is the best way to accurately cut the pattern pieces from fabric.

Freezer paper, if you haven't used it in quilting before, is a remarkable tool. This is ordinary freezer paper from the supermarket—not waxed paper or parchment paper. Freezer paper has a plain paper side and a shiny side. You can write on the paper side; then you place the shiny side down on the fabric and press gently with a warm iron, and it will melt just enough to adhere to the fabric. This allows you to cut along your drawn lines and accurately cut a piece of fabric that matches the pattern piece. Magic!

Lightbox or Other Light Source

The best way to trace onto freezer paper is with a lightbox, which you can buy in an art supply store or online. These are plastic boxes with a frosted Lucite top and a light inside, which makes it easy to see the pattern underneath the freezer paper. If you don't have a lightbox, don't worry. You can use painter's tape to tape your pattern to any window and then tape your freezer paper on top of that. Instant lightbox—but only during the day! If you have a glass-top table, you can put a lamp underneath it and use that as your lightbox. The goal is to have your pattern on top of your light source, freezer paper on top of the pattern, both facing up, and light coming through from the bottom. This allows you to see the lines in your pattern clearly so you can trace them onto the freezer paper.

tip

In a pinch, an iPad can be used as a small lightbox; download a "softbox" lighting app (I use a free app called Color Softbox and choose White Light). To protect the screen and keep the page from advancing, I purchased an 8″ × 10″ piece of Lucite from the frame department of an art supply store, which I place on top of the iPad. Adjust the brightness on the iPad to the highest point for maximum light.

TRACING ONTO FREEZER PAPER

Put the pattern faceup on the lightbox (or window) and place a piece of freezer paper on top of it with the paper side up. With a mechanical pencil, trace only the area of the dress—nothing else for now. This includes the overall outline and the lines that indicate where the different values are positioned. Write the value numbers on the freezer paper.

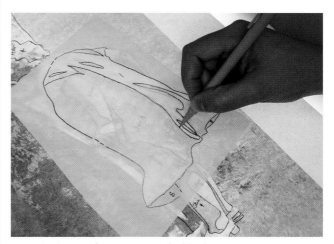

Trace the dress on freezer paper and add value numbers.

CUTTING AND LAYERING THE FABRIC PIECES

 1 Take the piece of freezer paper to your ironing board or pressing surface and lay your foundation fabric faceup. Place the freezer paper so the paper side is up and the shiny side is on the fabric. With your iron set on warm (cotton setting), press down on the freezer paper (don't move back and forth) and hold the iron in place for a second or two. Remove your iron and you will see that the freezer paper is stuck to the fabric.

NOTE

This is not a situation where you will be cutting the reverse side, as you might have learned for traditional appliqué.

You don't want it so stuck that you can't remove it or too lightly stuck so that it comes off when you lift the fabric; but if it isn't secure, give it another few seconds under the iron.

Press freezer paper to the foundation fabric.

 2 Turn off your iron and cut on the outline of the whole dress foundation, cutting both the fabric and the freezer paper.

> *tip*
>
> *I always recommend having a designated pair of small scissors for this part of the process because paper dulls the scissor blades. This is not the place to use your good fabric scissors.*

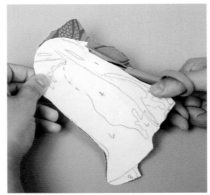

Cut around the outline of the dress.

3 Gently peel the fabric from the freezer paper—the tip of a straight pin can help get it started.

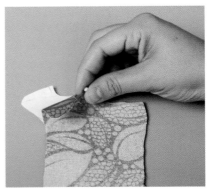

Peel fabric off the freezer paper.

Now you have your foundation and you are ready to cut the next value.

This is the foundation for the dress.

4 Use the same piece of freezer paper and press it onto the value 4 fabric. Carefully cut away any of the value 6 parts and use that remaining bit of freezer paper as your guide for placement. Then, do the same with the value 1 fabric. Finally those tiny bits of value 8 on the bottom of her skirt and at her sleeve are done last. Then the dress section of the girl is finished.

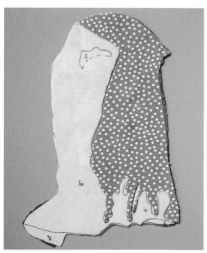

Use the cut-away piece of freezer paper to position the new layered piece of fabric.

All fabrics that make up the dress

tip

To cut those open little spots inside a pattern piece, fold the fabric in the center of the place you want to cut, make a small snip, open it, and use that snip to get your scissor in and cut out the section.

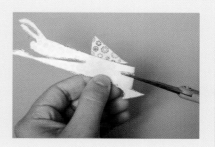

5 The next step is the sections of skin—her face, arms, and legs. Identify the fabrics you want to use. Make sure they all have the same underlying color tone and blend together nicely.

The face, each arm, and both legs together will be treated as separate sections.

 NOTE

Some areas of my freezer paper tracings have a dashed line rather than a solid line (on the top of the legs and on the partially visible arm). These areas will be placed underneath her dress, so I want to leave a little overlap, which will help me glue the pieces together. Instead of tracing exactly on the line at the edge of those pieces, I make the dashed line about ⅛" larger than the pattern piece. Solid lines are cut right on the line. Dashed lines do not need to be cut that accurately.

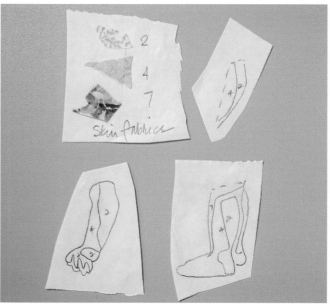

Skin sections and fabric guide

Since the majority of the skin area is value 4, it is a good foundation for the two arms and the legs. Set the face aside for now because we will complete it with her hair.

6 Trace the arms and the legs onto freezer paper and cut out the foundations for these sections. Then cut out the remaining values in each of the arms and the legs. Position these in the same way you positioned the pieces for the dress.

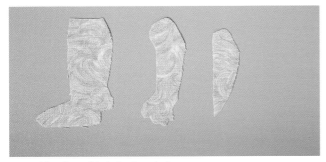

Start with value 4 fabric for foundation.

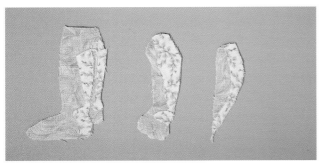

Add value 2 fabric.

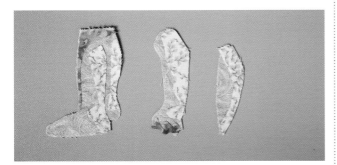

Finally, add the value 7 fabric.

The head is a single section that includes both skin tones and hair.

7 Identify the two hair fabrics (zingers are fun here) and use the value 9 fabric as the foundation for the entire head.

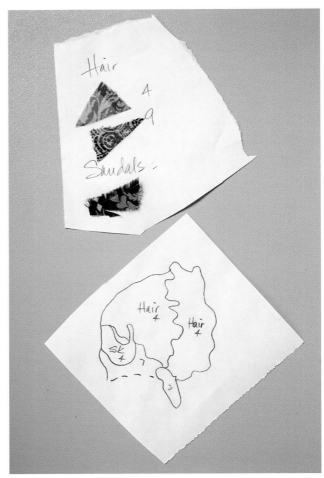

Head piece and fabric guide

▼▼▼ *tip*

You will have a lot of layering of fabric, but don't worry; this isn't a problem in most art quilts. If you are working on a very small piece and it becomes too bulky, just trim away some of the underneath layers to thin it out—but keep the foundation piece intact.

8 Cut and position the other hair piece and the small skin value 7 and the skin value 4 that provides the highlight on her face and ear. The last piece to add is the small value 2 skin fabric at the base of her neck.

Start with hair value 9 foundation fabric and add hair value 4 fabric.

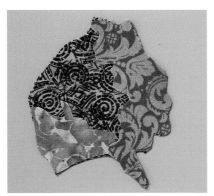

Skin value 7 added.

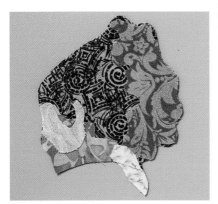

Skin values 4 and 2 added.

The last section of the girl is her sandals. In the photo they are white, but because their value does not need to relate to anything else, you can make them any color you wish. I wanted to use this pretty purple fabric; you can use whatever you like. You will notice on the pattern and original photo the sandals are a bit too big for her and stick out beyond her toe. This is not a detail that I thought added anything to the overall composition, so I ignored it. If you want to add that tiny dab of sandal in front of her toe, go for it.

9 Choose a fabric and cut out the girl's sandals.

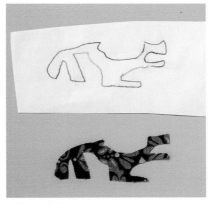

Girl's sandal

If you look closely, you will also see that when I cut the sandals I took a little liberty with the lines and cut them both as a single piece of fabric. This makes it much easier to place and won't be significant when the quilt is put together.

Finished girl

10 Step back and examine your girl.

Do you like the way she looks? Would you like to make any changes? See Evaluating Your Work (page 58) for ideas.

EVALUATING YOUR WORK

Looking at the Design

DIGITAL CAMERA   Looking at your work in progress on your computer is much better for instantly identifying something that isn't working than looking at it with your naked eye. Whenever I take a photo and display it on my computer screen, problems are more obvious.

BACKWARD BINOCULARS   Binoculars are designed to make something far away look closer, but when turned around to see something as it would look farther away, they are a great tool for evaluating your work. It is like stepping back across a large room, and any problems become much more apparent than when standing up close. You can also purchase a reducing glass (which looks like a magnifying glass but makes things look farther away).

FOAM CORE PORTABLE DESIGN WALL   I have a design wall in my studio onto which I pin all work in progress and step back to view it with my backward binoculars or reducing glass. Not everyone has the space for a design wall. What I recommend in that case is a sheet of foam core. Foam core has a Styrofoam center with poster board on either side. Art stores, and even office supply stores, sell foam core in a variety of sizes. Choose a size that is larger than the art quilt you are working on and you can use it as your work surface, pin your work to it, and then stand it up on a piece of furniture and step back to view and evaluate it. Even a smaller piece of foam core will allow you to work on one element at a time and stand it up to evaluate. Remember: Before lifting your foam core to a vertical position, each little fabric piece needs a pin to hold it in place.

Solutions

It has been my experience that when something doesn't look right, it is almost always a question of value. If one of the values is off, the whole element looks awkward. Stepping back to evaluate will allow you to see which of the fabric pieces might be the wrong value—usually because two areas blend into each other and look like one large section, or because the jump between values is too extreme.

Another common problem is the color tone, especially with skin tones. Fabrics that looked like they would play nicely together on your worktable sometimes just don't work when you put them together and look at them, often because they have different undertones.

Sometimes, one fabric might demand too much attention compared with the others. This can be distracting and is particularly common with a zinger. If the zinger is used in an area that becomes a focal point, or is too large, it can be a distraction rather than an asset. Moving it to a smaller area of the element can often solve the problem. If that doesn't work, the offending fabric needs to be replaced for the good of the rest.

Finally, the placement of a part of the element might be off, which can make everything look wrong, especially when the placement is critical—like facial features.

Especially when depicting body language, the position of every section that makes up the figure is important, so I use a tracing paper template to double-check.

My little girl isn't quite right, and the problem is the placement of the sections. I can use a tracing paper template to double-check.

Tracing Paper Template

Use tracing paper to trace around the girl and the major value changes in the pattern. No detail is needed, just a quick overall view. You can see when I place this tracing onto the fabric girl I am working on, my problem is that her head and legs are in the wrong position. That wonderful curiosity expressed by the body language in the photo is lost because the head is not positioned properly. I gently lift the tracing paper template and use a straight pin to nudge the pieces until they are directly under the corresponding part of the template. What a difference a little tweaking makes.

Tracing from the pattern.

Line up the sections of the element with the traced pattern.

Use a pin to nudge the pieces into place under the tracing paper.

The little girl looks right now.

GLUING THE PIECES

When you like the way your element looks, you need to glue the pieces together.

1 Squeeze a bit of fabric glue onto a scrap of freezer paper.

2 Using the tip of a toothpick, dab little tiny bits of glue under the fabric pieces, just enough to hold everything in place.

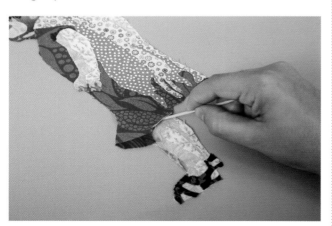

Remember, you have a lot of layers in some spots, so glue all layers down. This is a good time to trim some from underneath if you think it is too bulky.

3 Set aside your first finished element.

The Boy

The boy is another element, broken into five sections: head, both arms (one is very dark and almost hidden between his legs), pants, shirt, and finally shoes.

The steps to making the boy are similar to making the girl. Refer to The Girl (pages 50–60) for more detailed information.

 1 Starting with the pants, determine the values needed for the fabrics. This is already on the pattern for you.

NOTE

Remember that the full-size pattern I've provided is lighter than the original. Use the original GIMP pattern (page 48) to determine value numbers for yourself or just use the value numbers I've provided.

I have decided to stay with blue, but you can use any color you want. Look at a lot of possibilities and narrow the selection to those with the correct values.

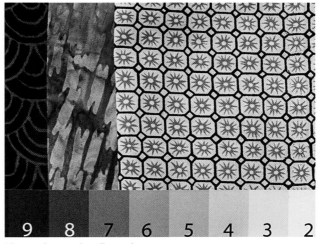

9 8 7 6 5 4 3 2

These colors work well together.

Because they will make up most of the boy's body, I want to choose the shirt fabrics and the pant fabrics at the same time. Although some of the values are the same in both the pants and the shirt, I try not to use the same fabrics in both places. Using a different fabric in each element—and even in each section—is less confusing visually, especially if they are the same color.

2 Prepare the chart and trace the sections onto freezer paper.

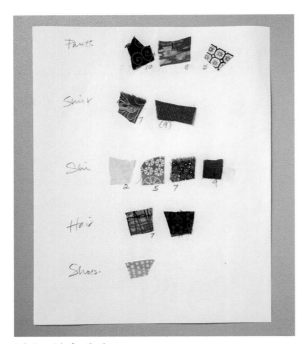

Fabric guide for the boy

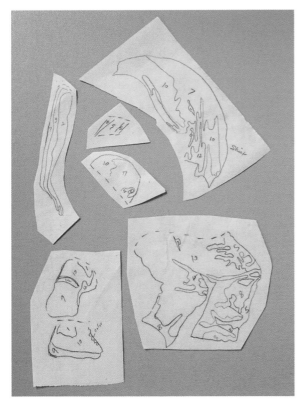

Trace sections onto freezer paper.

You can either trace all of them at once or trace them as you go—it makes no difference. Notice where I have put the solid lines and the dashed lines on my freezer paper tracings; remember that the dashed lines do not need to be accurately cut, although the solid lines do.

Make the boy's pants the same way you made the girl's dress.

3 Start with the foundation.

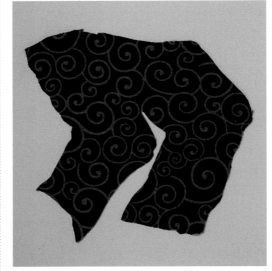

Foundation fabric, value 10

4 Add the next fabric.

Add second fabric, value 8.

5 Add the third fabric.

Add third fabric, value 5.

The shirt is made the same way and then placed next to the pants to see how they look together.

6 Position the first two shirt fabrics.

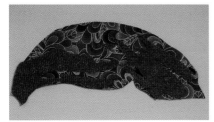

Values 10 and 7

I've noticed that something isn't working with the fabric choices I made (see When Things Don't Work as Planned, at right).

WHEN THINGS DON'T WORK AS PLANNED

When I chose the shirt fabrics, I liked the way this dark blue fabric looked with the print, so I decided to use it even though its value number was a little lower than the pattern indicated. But it doesn't look right. The shadow area on the shirt really does need to be closer to the value of the shadow area on the pants (A).

The darker value looks better, but now I think the other fabric on the shirt demands too much attention (B). Changing to one with some surface interest but not such a strong print will be less distracting (C).

A. Value of the shadow on his shirt is too light.

B. A darker value of the shadow on the shirt works better, but the other shirt fabric is too distracting.

C. The shirt fabric was changed to a print that demands less attention and added value 12 for the dark shadows.

7 The final step is to add the dark shadowy areas—value 12 that appears on his shirt and pants.

8 Build the shoes, arm, and head sections the same way. Remember to add extra fabric to pieces that need to be overlapped.

- His extended arm is built on the value 5 foundation.
- The dark arm behind him is built on the value 9 foundation.
- The head is built on the value 7 hair fabric foundation.
- The shoes are built on the value 10 foundation.

Shoe, arm, and head sections

9 Now the boy is complete. If you are unsure of the placement of the sections, make a tracing paper template (see Tracing Paper Template, page 59) for him to make sure everything is in the right place. Glue the layers together.

NOTE

Sometimes when the areas are very close in value or too small to cut, I eliminate them entirely. Just blend the area into the adjacent area and forget it. Remember, the pattern is just your guide; you can make adjustments whenever you think it is necessary. For example, the shoes are so dark that I didn't bother with the shadows.

The Tree

Now that you have successfully completed the girl and boy, you can turn your attention to the tree. You can see on the pattern that I have designated a fairly simple rendition of the values in the tree by breaking it down to only 3 fabrics—values 3, 7, and 10—plus a spot of dark fabric for the hole in the tree trunk. I have chosen a dark brown that has light and dark areas for value 10; look for a fabric that reads more like a solid than one with a lot of pattern. I paired that with the two lighter values that each have a little more going on in the print for values 3 and 7.

1 For the foundation of the tree, use the value 10 fabric.

2 Layer all three of the values to form the basic tree in exactly the same way you created the girl and boy. Add the hole piece.

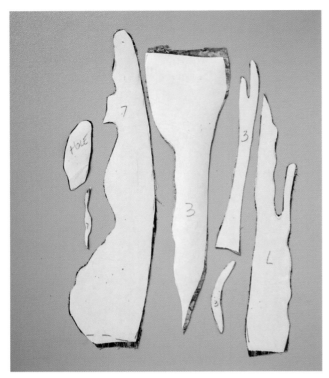

Tree pieces cut out

Tree foundation with 4 fabrics

3 Now add some zingers. If you would like to leave the tree the way it is, you certainly can—but you have the opportunity to go a little wild with fabric and really make this your own.

I love to use zinger fabrics in trees. A tree has so much texture that adding unexpected fabric selections is almost mandated. Look at my chart; you can see the three fabrics I used for the basic tree and six zingers that will add life and excitement. Two are light in value, two are medium, and two are darker.

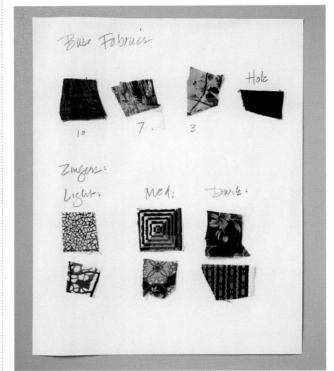

Fabric guide for the tree

I don't bother to assign value numbers for two reasons—first, zingers are hard to pin down as a single value; and second, these fabrics are "extra," and therefore their values do not need to correspond directly to anything in the pattern. The only factor I consider is their color—in my case I am staying in the brown family, with the exception of a yellow and orange African fabric and a dark green geometric, both of which will really make this tree extra special when used sparingly.

Starting with the darker values, cut random pieces of your two dark zingers and lay them where the pattern would suggest the tree is darker. This is not a science; move the pieces around so they are equally distributed around the tree and you like the way they look. Use the original photo as a guide for the placement of the darker fabrics. Less is more with zingers; you only need some irregularly cut narrow strips and not too many of them.

Do the same with your medium-value zingers, placing them where they will transition from the darker areas of the pattern to the lighter areas. Move them around, step back, and evaluate. Make note of where the boy and girl will be—there is no point in carefully placing zingers in the areas of the tree that will be covered by the figures. A rough tracing onto tracing paper will give you a basic idea of where they will overlap the tree.

Add medium-value zingers.

Add dark zingers.

Finally, add your lighter zingers to the areas of the tree in sunlight. Not many are needed, as most of the tree is dark. Here, I have used only a few pieces of the African fabric and the one with the crackle texture. You do not want to add so many zingers that the original three tree fabrics are lost— the zingers should serve as an accent, not the main event. Look at the way I have completed the tree, but then close your book and do it your way. This is your chance to use the zingers you like and put them where you want. Have fun. When you are happy with your tree, glue the pieces.

Add light zingers.

Adding the Surrounding Environment

Most of the work is done. In the original photo, there is a wall in the background with advertising, which I do not want to include in my quilt. If you want to include it, simply follow the pattern and treat the wall as you would any other element. I want the focus of attention to be on the beautiful tree and the two children, so I simplified the background.

1   Choose the fabric for the grass.

2   Add the shadows on the grass alongside the children's feet.

Add shadows.

3 Cut small pieces that resemble high grass to add in front of the children's feet. This will make the grass more realistic and soften the edges where they are standing *in* the grass, rather than *on* the grass.

Cut grass pieces.

Place grass pieces around feet.

4 The only thing left for your art quilt top is a fabric that will serve as the sky. Keep it simple and light in color.

Now you are ready to finish your quilt.

CHOOSING HORIZON LINE AND AUDITIONING GRASS FABRICS

Although the horizon line (where the grass meets the sky) is fairly high in the original photo, I think it distracts attention, so I am going to place it lower. If you want your horizon line higher in the composition, put it where you think it looks best.

Lower horizon line

High horizon line

Look at the fabric options I have pinned to my design wall to compare. I have decided my first instinct is the one I like best—the color isn't too dark and the texture is appropriate.

Both the color and the print in this fabric seem overpowering.

The color is good, but the texture feels wrong.

The texture here is better, but the color seems a little dull.

The color is bright and the texture is lost.

FINISHING YOUR ART QUILT

Batting or No Batting

Art quilts have their origins in traditional quilting, and for years this meant that art quilters retained many of the techniques and materials of traditional bed quilts. But in recent years, even exhibitions that used to require "a top and bottom layer with batting in the middle, held together by stitching" have relaxed their definition of what constitutes an art quilt.

No longer bound by traditional quilting "rules," art quilters are free to explore and produce their work in any way that makes sense to the individual artist. I, for one, have left batting by the wayside. You may choose to do the same—or not—it is all up to you.

As my artistic voice has evolved in the years since I began making art quilts, I have been moving more and more toward a hard-edged, graphic art look; and batting, with its ups and downs, shadows and puffiness, doesn't fit the bill for me. I also no longer enjoy doing all the decorative stitching that many art quilters so enjoy—and do so well.

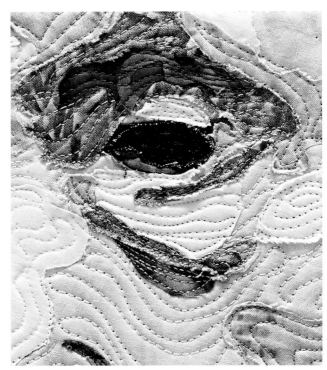

Free-motion quilting with a batting layer adds shadows and puffiness. Detail of *Old Woman* (full quilt on page 23).

Functional stitching holds the pieces together and, in a quilt without batting, looks flatter. Detail of *Shadow Puppets* (full quilt on page 108).

So if you are like me, you can skip the batting. The result is a flatter-looking quilt without any stitching requirements beyond the purely functional stitches that hold the fabric collage pieces together. However, if you are one of those who loves sitting at your machine lost in the Zen of free-motion stitching, then batting is for you.

If you do use batting in your art quilt, choose one that is a "traditional" weight or thinner, not one with a high loft. Every piece of fabric you have glued to your quilt top will eventually need to be sewn down, and all those little pieces on a thick batting can create a jumble of shadows and puffy spots that will not be an advantage to your artwork.

When I do use batting, I work a little differently than many other art quilters. I stitch all the pieces down on the batting alone without a backing fabric. Once the stitching is completed, a clean fabric back is added and the edges are finished. The truth is, the stitching can be done before or after the back is added. It really doesn't matter—you decide.

Backing Fabric

For quilts with batting, I use good-quality muslin for the quilt back. I purchase high-quality off-white muslin or solid cotton by the bolt, so I always have it on hand. All my pieces are the same color on the back, and that continuity appeals to me; plus I never have to search for a piece of fabric from my stash that is big enough but I won't miss somewhere down the line.

For quilts without batting, I use cotton canvas for the backing fabric. Canvas is heavier than standard cotton fabric, so the art quilt has nice body and hangs well even without the batting. The quilt top is placed onto the canvas and the functional stitching is done onto both. But be warned, most cotton canvas is not preshrunk, so press it first with a steam iron before you use it. I can actually see the fabric shrink up under the iron as I press. Take a look through the art quilts in this book (you will be able to tell which have the batting in them and which do not) and then you can decide for yourself which look you prefer. Or better yet, try it both ways—then decide.

Functional Sewing

Whether or not you are using batting, the stitching of all the little fabric pieces is the same. I use clear monofilament thread on the top of the machine and white in the bobbin. In the bobbin, I choose either a bobbin thread or a lingerie thread, something thin that will blend into the muslin or canvas and disappear—and won't pop up onto the quilt top.

If you are not familiar with monofilament thread, it comes in two colors—clear and smoke. Clear has no color and will not show on most fabrics; however, it is reflective, and on dark fabrics you can see the glimmer of the thread on the surface. Smoke monofilament is slightly gray, so it won't show on darker fabrics—but it will on light fabrics. You should always have both on hand, as most art quilts will require both to secure your fabric pieces.

Some quilters use the monofilament on the top of the machine and in the bobbin, but I do not. Monofilament is a little slippery and will grab nicely onto a standard thread. When used exclusively, it doesn't always grab as well, which can result in skipped stitches and tension issues. When using two different threads in the top and bobbin of your machine, you may need to adjust the tension—do a test on similarly layered fabrics to make sure nothing pops through on the bottom or top of your work.

The easiest way to accomplish your functional sewing is to use free-motion stitching with a darning foot and dropped feed dogs on your machine. Don't panic at the mere mention of free-motion. It isn't hard, and since you are only securing your pieces with clear thread, no one will know if it isn't perfect.

Start near the center of your quilt and use a zigzag stitch setting on your machine. Gently guide your needle along the edge of the fabric pieces, encasing the edges in the zigzag stitch. Finish the clear thread areas and change to the smoke thread to complete the edges of the dark fabrics. Free-motion means you can move back and forth, side to side, and roll along without having to pivot and lift the needle every time you want to turn. The more you do it, the easier it will be.

Free-motion stitching

When all the pieces are sewn in place, you can add decorative quilt stitching if you wish. Skies and other large areas are great places to show off your stitching talents. If you are working on a very large art quilt, you may have to do some stitching within broad cuts of fabric so that they don't sag over time. The rule of thumb is the same as it is for traditional quilts—stitching every 4", or about the width of your relaxed hand.

Press your art quilt so that all the threads relax, and trim the edges, if necessary, to square it off.

Edge Finishing

There are many ways to finish the edges of an art quilt. You may already have a favorite. Many art quilters use a standard binding or a "pillowcase edge," and if that is what you like, you can find a lot of information in books and online about how to do both.

I prefer to keep it simple and usually finish my quilts in one of two ways—either a zigzag stitch with monofilament thread, which protects the edges from fraying, or stretched onto canvas stretchers.

The zigzag is about as simple as you can get, and this is the best choice if you want your finished art quilt to have a shape that isn't a square or rectangle. Set the machine on zigzag (you can use your walking foot now and pop your feed dogs back up) to encase the raw edges of your art quilt.

Zigzag-stitched edge

Canvas stretchers are available in any store that sells art supplies and are fairly inexpensive. They come in 1" increments and are sold separately, so remember to always buy them in pairs. Say, for example, your finished art quilt will be 18" × 24"; you will need to purchase two each of 18" stretchers and 24" stretchers.

1 The stretchers are designed to nestle together at the corners. Put the 4 pieces together to form the desired size and use your rotary ruler or a T-square to make sure the corners are at right angles and everything is straight and squared.

2 Use a staple gun to put a single staple across the diagonal seam at each corner to keep the stretchers from wiggling around.

3 Trim your quilt top 3" larger on each side than the finished art quilt.

4 Position your quilt top facedown on the table and put the stretcher "square" on top of it.

5 Start by pulling the top of the art quilt onto the top stretcher and put one staple in the center. Now pull the bottom onto the stretcher and put a single staple in the center. Flip it over to the front and make sure it looks even and straight. This is the time to make adjustments—not after all the staples are in.

6 Turn it back over to the back, pull each side taut, and put a single staple in each center.

7 Double-check the front. If it looks right, flip it over to the back, pull the top taut, and staple across the top first and then the bottom. Give the fabric enough of a tug to ensure a nice, tight surface, but not so hard that you distort it. Now pull and staple the sides.

8 To complete each corner, flatten the remaining piece of fabric across the corner and tuck the ends in as you would when wrapping a gift. This takes a little bit of maneuvering, but after you get the hang of it, it really isn't hard. Staple your corners in place and you are done.

First fold of corner

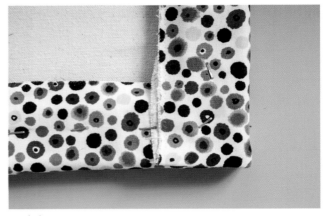

Stapled corner

Second fold of corner

Back of stretchers

Staple in place

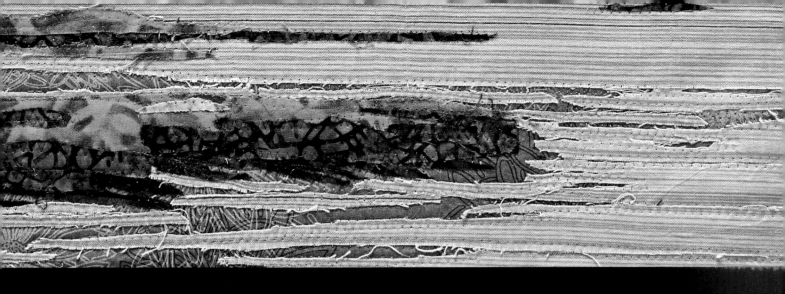

SECTION THREE
TIPS AND TRICKS
FOR COMMON ELEMENTS

In this section, I will give you some rules of thumb for creating common elements in your art quilts. These are only meant as a guide; you can explore, experiment, and decide for yourself how best to accomplish what you want in your own art quilts.

For each element I will show you how to use one, two, or three and more fabrics. Different compositions will require different approaches, as will the finished size of your art quilt and the level of detail you wish to depict. I will show you how to improvise beyond the pattern to let loose and have some fun with fabric.

Anything organic (found in nature) can be accomplished in fabric without having to follow the pattern exactly. Trees are all different, water changes constantly, leaves blend together—so these are not elements in your art quilt that require specific and individual details. Consequently, these are areas where you can let loose and play a little.

In this section I will outline how to accomplish each element using one fabric, three fabrics, or a multitude of fabrics. You make the decision. The pattern is still your guide to shape, light, and shadow, but the rest is all up to you.

Trees

The most important thing to keep in mind when depicting a tree in fabric is the light source. In some photos, the trees are lit from either the front or the back, which means there is no light area and no shadow area—the overall tree looks to be the same value. But when the tree is lit from the side (as is often the case), you will have highlights and shadow.

In order to depict a tree using only one fabric, look for a fabric with a lot of visual interest. I love to use unexpected prints and patterns, fabrics with writing on them, and multicolored batiks. If you are using a print with a strong "line" to it (anything with an orientation) be sure to run the print vertically—to accent the vertical nature of the tree. If you run the pattern horizontally, the tree will look unnatural.

Detail of *Landscape, Winter* (full quilt on page 19)

Batik fabrics are a great way to depict a tree with light and shadow using a single fabric. Because batiks have highs and lows in the color, you can find a light area and center your freezer paper so the light part of the fabric is aligned with the light part of the tree.

Using two fabrics to create a tree requires a foundation fabric in a medium value and the highlighted area in a lighter value. This is where zingers can add some punch to your art quilt (see Zingers, page 25). Adding just a strip of the lighter value where the pattern indicates will give the tree dimension.

When using three or more fabrics, you want to use light, medium, and dark fabrics for your tree (see The Tree, pages 65–68). The medium value becomes your foundation and forms the center. The light fabrics go in the light areas and the dark values go on the shadow side. Mark the light, medium, and dark areas roughly on your freezer paper pattern and use them as a guide to cut your fabric pieces. Since bark is irregular, perfection isn't necessary.

Personally, I love a lot of different fabrics in my trees; this is an opportunity to use zingers and make a statement. Choose unexpected patterns, mix them together in little strips, and move them around until you have something that looks good to you. Remember, even when using multiple fabrics, vary the print scales, position directional fabrics in a vertical orientation, and place the lighter fabrics on the lit side of the tree.

Detail of *Landscape, Winter* (full quilt on page 19)

Detail of *Explorers* (full quilt on page 40)

Leaves

Leaves can all be cut individually, but it will probably make you crazy. Instead, find a fabric that has variations in color that will appear to be more complex when placed in the area of the leaves. Placing lighter-colored fabrics toward the front and darker fabrics behind will give the impression of shadows behind the leaves. This is not a place to use gently curving cuts; jagged edges will appear more natural.

Iola Birches

Grass

Some fabrics resemble grass, but I tend not to use them. They are usually the wrong scale, the wrong perspective, or just look too contrived. Instead, look for fabric that has a nice perceived texture and variations in color. Look at your photo to see where the shadows are and use darker fabrics in the appropriate value. Shadows should be approximately the size and shape shown in your photo, but accuracy isn't necessary. Color will have an impact on the mood or season of your quilt. Spring grass is lighter and has more yellow in it, summer grass is a deeper green; and moving into autumn you will need a combination of browns, yellows, greens, and oranges.

Detail of *Landscape, Summer* (full quilt on page 18)

Detail of *Explorers* (full quilt on page 40)

Water

Often, a single fabric can be found that has striations in it that are reminiscent of water. Make sure that any fabric with an obvious orientation is placed horizontally. Keep in mind that water is not always blue—often it is closer to gray or even brown, depending on the surrounding light. Don't assume that blue is the right color—look at your photo to see what the color really is. Remember: Use your eyes, not your brain. Even though your brain will tell you water is always blue, your eye knows better.

When using a single fabric, often nothing else is required. Batiks work well for water; the light and dark areas resemble movement. Any fabric with striations or lines that can be placed horizontally will look like water; broken lines are more interesting than straight ones. If the fabric you choose for the water is lighter on the back, this can make a good "highlight" on the water and can even look like small whitecaps, giving movement and reflection to your water. When water is calm, even a small stripe can be an interesting choice.

Detail of *Landscape, Fall* (full quilt on page 19)

In *Pails and Shovels*, the water is just the background and did not demand much attention, so a single fabric was enough. Here, I decided the front of the fabric was too blue, so I used the back instead. The subtle striations of the fabric and the highlighted areas (dark this time) are actually the front of the fabric, cut in little strips and randomly placed, giving the sense that the water is calm.

For *Shifting Tide*, I used a batik as the base of the water, which already had a lot of movement and visual interest. Then I used a white fabric as the whitecaps. I couldn't use the back of the fabric for highlights because batiks are the same value on both sides. These pieces were randomly cut, paying attention to the photo for the approximate size and shape of the whitecaps and their placement, particularly around the rocks.

Pails and Shovels

Detail of *Shifting Tide*
(full quilt on page 85)

Detail of *Purple Seascape*
(full quilt on page 86)

When depicting water using three fabrics, I choose a water base color, a lighter highlight color, and a shadow color. This isn't usually necessary when looking at long ocean views, but it is helpful for water up against the side of rocks or a boat or another object—anywhere a shadow will be cast onto the water. Again, look at the photo to see where these darker areas appear and cut and place little snips of fabric until you like the way the shadows appear on the water.

Rapidly moving water provides opportunities to have some fun with multiple fabrics. Unexpected choices can turn a photo into a real work of art. *Icy Perch* was made to celebrate moving water, which is the focal point. If you look closely at the fabrics used, many of them are not fabrics that would say "water" on their own. But when used in a variety of values and cut in irregular curving pieces (rather than hard-edged strips), they come together to resemble the movement of water. The zingers (there are quite a few) seem to blend in and add some visual excitement to the rest of the choices (see Zingers, page 25). It is important that all the fabric pieces move in the same direction, just the way water would move in one direction—in this case on a diagonal, which also adds to the sense of movement. I wanted to give the illusion of a very cold place, so I used clear blues (a cool color) combined with true white, using color temperature (see Color Temperature, page 10) to enhance the appearance of ice and cold.

Icy Perch

Rocks

Rocks may seem difficult, but they are not. As with tree bark, the most important thing to keep in mind is where the light and shadows lie on the rock surface. Rocks are rarely all one color, and they usually have a lot of dips in the surface. Because all rock is irregular, it isn't necessary to follow your pattern exactly.

Often, you can find a batik or a print fabric with variations in color that will work alone for small areas of rock in your composition. For two fabrics,

cut the foundation from your main fabric and add another darker fabric for the shadow areas. When the rock is a featured part of your composition, three or more fabrics will work best.

Use your freezer paper tracing to note where most of the light and the shadows occur. Create the foundation using a middle-value fabric—something with highs and lows in the print that will resemble rock. Add the light values and dark values, using more jagged-shaped

Detail of *Man Standing Looking at Mountain* (full quilt below)

pieces than smooth curves, and using your photo as an approximate guide to where they should be placed. You do not want huge jumps in value, and a few larger pieces are better than a lot of little ones.

Distance

Mountains (or anything for that matter) that recede into the distance become grayer (less saturated) and lighter in color the farther back they are from the foreground. They are usually cool colors like blue, purple, or green rather than warm; but the farther away the mountain is, the lighter it will be. This is not a place for prints or zingers; it is one of the few places I use solid or almost-solid fabrics. A pattern in the fabric will bring the element forward visually, contradicting the distance you are attempting to create.

You can use a single fabric for distant mountains only if there is one line of mountains in the background. The illusion of far-receding mountains can be accomplished only with multiple fabrics, moving from darker in the front to lighter in the back. Every time the peaks move farther into the distance, another fabric is required.

Man Standing Looking at Mountain, inspired by a photo by Linda Beach

Sky

Many art quilters do a lot of piece-work to create the illusion of sky, but I am not one of them. Personally, I like the foreground to tell the story, so unless the sky is the star of the show, I tend to find a fabric that I can use in a single piece. I am partial to light, striated, batik-type fabrics that will appear to be more intricate than they are. In *Landscape, Winter*, I used a swirling gray on white, which makes it look like a windy sky. In *Lizard*, I used a more whimsical fabric. Remember, sky is not always blue (as your brain would tell you); often it appears almost white.

Some hand-dyed or hand-painted fabrics are made specifically to look like sky, and some of these are quite beautiful. But those are an interpretation of sky done by another person, so I tend not to use them. Two fabrics for the sky would mean using a lighter fabric (or the back of your sky fabric) to designate cloud areas. Three or more fabrics would be used the same way you would depict water, with gently curving shapes and slight incremental changes in value.

Detail of *Landscape, Winter*
(full quilt on page 19)

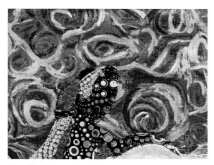

Detail of *Lizard*
(full quilt on page 90)

The fabric used for the sky in *Shifting Tide* is almost solid and fairly light.

Unexpected colors and pattern are used in *Purple Seascape*, such as the dotted fabric of the sky.

ANIMALS

Animals are a popular subject, whether exotic or just the beloved family pet. The key to bringing an animal to life is no different from any of the other compositional elements we have explored in this book, but the choice of fabric here is based very much on perceived texture. If the animal is only a small element of your quilt, a single fabric may suffice; but if the animal is the star of your art quilt, multiple fabrics will be necessary.

When making an art quilt of an animal, and particularly when doing a pet portrait, the starting photo is the key to a successful final product. Look for a compelling photo that captures the personality of your pet, or consider cropping in close to the face for a stronger composition. An animal will look better if the composition is pleasing, if there is some whimsy to the pose, or if the face fills the frame.

Photo by author

This photo of my little dog, Yendrik, will be a better art quilt if I crop in close to his face.

Fur

Yendrik

Fur is a perfect example of the importance of perceived texture. An animal with long curly fur, like a dog, will be best interpreted using fabrics with a lot of curving lines and shapes with a lot of little jigs and jags.

Animals with short straight fur will require a different kind of fabric. Here, curving or curlicue lines will be confusing. Fur that is flat and straight provides an opportunity to use unexpected prints.

Try to avoid obvious choices like leopard or zebra prints; opt instead for fabrics that will bring a hint of whimsy or surprise.

Feathers

Surprisingly, many of the fabrics I use for feathers are the same fabrics I use for water. Feathers are long and straight; therefore, the same types of prints that would give horizontal movement to water will do the same when used vertically or diagonally for feathers. Look at the feathers in the parrot—this is the same fabric used for the water in *Landscape, Fall* (page 19).

Parrot

Fabrics used in *Parrot*

Saturation becomes particularly important when working with birds. Tropical birds will require strong, bold, saturated colors, while northern species will look more natural with less-saturated color. Zingers are great fun when working with birds, because the pattern can add a lot of personality. Look at *Bluejay* and the corresponding fabrics used—not necessarily what you might have expected for a bird. Notice that I used both the front and back of the solid gray fabric for two different values.

Bluejay, inspired by a photo by Sue Freebern

Fabrics used in *Bluejay*

Beaks and Feet

Unless the bird is very large and detailed, I try to use a single fabric for the beak and a single fabric for the feet (see *Parrot*, page 88, and *Bluejay*, page 89). Beaks are smooth and can be effectively done with one fabric, perhaps with some changes in value, fussy cut to put the lighter areas in the places where light is reflected. Often, though, the beak is simply a color that adds punch on its own, and finding the right color and value is all you need to do.

Birds' feet are as varied as the types of birds. Some are smooth and some are not. Look for a texture in a fabric that seems reminiscent of the texture in the photo—or use a zinger (see Zingers, page 25).

Reptiles

Lizard, inspired by a photo by Aaron Epstein

I will admit that I have a personal fondness for reptiles—not necessarily in life but certainly in art. The texture of reptile skin is so wonderful and lends itself to the use of interesting fabrics that simply wouldn't work for a dog or a cat.

Unlike the curvy prints for fur and the striated prints for feathers, here you want to look for fabrics with irregular and circular prints—and the more the merrier.

Eyes

Most animals have eyes that appear to be black, which makes them fairly easy to do using a single dark fabric. Remember: If a spot of light is reflected from a light source into an animal's eyes (as frequently seen with human eyes), this will add life to your art quilt. If the reflected light isn't in the photo, you don't need it in your art quilt.

Cats, both wild and domestic, have eyes that are usually a strong and dramatic color and can be the focal point of any close-up of a cat's face. Here, I always recommend exaggerating the actual eye color by pumping up the volume just a bit—use a fabric that is the right color but is more saturated or brighter than the real eye might appear. And don't forget that light source!

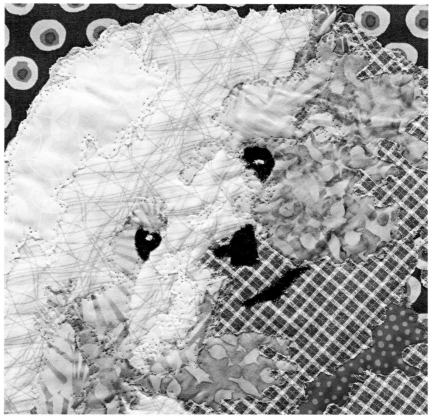

Detail of *Yendrik* (full quilt on page 87)

 tip

Use your eyes, not your brain! For snapshots with flash, you might get a yellow or red eye. Obviously that is not the color you would want to choose. Look at your pet to determine the actual color.

PEOPLE

Faces might seem intimidating, but the principal technique is the same as for any other element. Unlike organic elements, however, a portrait in fabric requires more precise placement of all pieces. Little details really matter—an eye that slants ⅛" down or is ¼" too far from the nose will essentially look like another person.

There is nothing inherently more difficult about a face than any other element in an art quilt. The pattern is prepared the same way, fabrics are chosen the same way, and in the end, the construction is done the same way. Using a tracing paper template is helpful to ensure that everything is exactly where it belongs.

Skin Tones

One of the greatest challenges while making art quilts of people is finding fabric for the skin tones. Beige and brown fabrics often have an underlying color tone, which means they can look slightly blue, yellow, or red (see Gray, Beige, and Taupe, page 16). Too red and the skin looks unnaturally ruddy; too yellow and the face will look sickly. If you combine beiges that work in value but have different

Old Man, inspired by a photo by Lin Hsin-Chen

underlying color tones, they will not blend together to look like the contours of a face. If the difference in values is too little, the face may appear to be done with only a single fabric, without contour or shadow. On the other hand, big jumps between values may look choppy.

I create a lot of faces in my art quilts, which is why I am always shopping for beige fabrics. This does not mean solid fabrics, I love using unexpected patterns like geometrics and florals in a face. These add life and interest; I just need to make sure they all have the same underlying color and the values move from light to dark as they appear in the pattern. Look at the fabric choices in the face of *Old Man*; most of these are a far cry from solid beige fabrics.

Ethnicity does not matter when choosing fabric. Even a pale skin color will have brown tones in the shadowy areas; darker skin tones will simply start farther along the value scale. The key is finding the same values as your pattern.

Couple on the Beach

The choice of color can set the mood of the face in your quilt, as with any other element in an art quilt, although the color choice is much more subtle with skin tones. A young child made in fabric with yellow undertones will look unhealthy; an older person in pink-beige tones may look flushed. When you move away from realistic color, however, you can set an entirely different mood with color, like in *Old Woman*. Here the blue and purple colors lend a cool detachment to a face that is not warm and friendly. Remember, this is not a photographic portrait—it is art, so there are no limits to your interpretation.

Old Woman

In *Jagged*, I used black-and-white prints with purple, which sets an entirely different mood. Drawing attention to that jagged line makes the face just a little unnerving. The result is artwork, not a portrait of a particular person.

Jagged

If the face you wish to convey is not someone specific (I take a lot of photos of strangers and do not want to make them recognizable) or if the face is not the focus of your art quilt, you do not need to use much detail at all. In *In Her Footsteps*, the faces of the two girls were not important to the overall composition (nor were they particularly large), allowing me to fussy cut a single batik fabric that gave a sense of the contours and shadows without making this a portrait of these two girls.

Detail of *In Her Footsteps* (full quilt on page 105)

In *After*, however, the simplification was intentional. Creating a pattern with only two values in the face results in a strong and graphic image rather than a portrait, and it required only two fabrics (plus the black for the eyes).

Detail of *After* (full quilt on page 42)

For *In the Moment*, I reduced the face and neck to just three skin tones: a light, a medium, and a dark, although they do not stray far from each other in value. But look at the prints on these three fabrics—not what you might expect to use as human skin.

Detail of *In the Moment* (full quilt on page 41)

The greater the detail you require (and the larger the face in the finished art quilt), the more fabric values you will need. Look closely at *Bittersweet*, where I added a geometric zinger for just a hint of something different; in *Morning Paper*, I used geometrics and florals. In *Old Man* (page 92), I used a lot of zingers, but because the tones and values are correct, it works.

Detail of *Bittersweet* (full quilt on page 100)

Detail of *Morning Paper*
(full quilt on page 101)

Eyes

An eye needs to have strong contrast and can effectively be done using just black (or another very dark color) and white, as shown in several of the faces in this section. Even though the human eye is not really white or black, the exaggeration of the strong contrast draws attention to that part of the face.

Detail of *After* (full quilt on page 42)

We have all heard the expression "The eyes are the window to the soul," and never was that more true than in the gorgeous photo *Afghan Girl* taken by Steve McCurry (used here with his generous permission). The eyes of the Afghan girl are the most important feature of this image, so to translate them into fabric, it is important to really examine the eye color. In this case, the eyes are actually three colors—a very deep blue around the edges, moving into a teal blue and a golden tone, with of course black and white. The size of the finished quilt will determine the level of detail in the eyes, and a smaller quilt would necessitate simplifying the number of colors used.

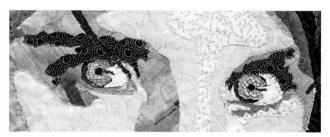
Detail of eye in *Afghan Girl* (full quilt on page 110)

A face is always more striking if the eye color is exaggerated just a bit. Although the white of a human eye is not really white, nor is the black truly black, the eyes will look more dramatic if done that way in fabric. By the same token, exaggerating the eye color itself just a bit will draw attention to the eyes and make them the focal point.

The most important thing to remember is to add the light source to an eye. Human eyes always reflect the light, which illuminates them. When looking at professional photos of people, you can actually tell what sort of lighting was used, because the size and shape of the light source is reflected in the eyes. In the photo *Afghan Girl*, the light source looks like two elongated triangles; often it is just a small circle or strip of white. Without this reflection of the light source, the eye will look lifeless. Just a tiny dot of white fabric is often all that is needed. Your original photo will show you when and where to place the highlight.

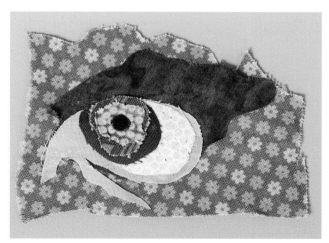
This eye lacks the white reflection and looks lifeless.

Lips

Lips illustrate the principle "Use your eyes, not your brain." Our brain tells us that lips are red or pink, but this is usually true only if the person is wearing lipstick. If you really look at the lips in your starting photo, you will see that they are more often a variation of the skin tones, with perhaps just a hint of a pinkish tone. Lips look most natural if there is contour—since lips are rounded, they will have areas of highlight and shadow. Showing the highlight will accent the fullness and roundness of the lips. Lips can be effectively done using nothing more than the skin tone values you use for the rest of the face—especially for men.

For single-fabric lips, a trick I love is to fussy cut an area from a large floral or any fabric with light and dark areas. For lips, I find a flower petal that has some light, medium, and dark in it and position the freezer paper template over the fabric (sometimes it helps to do this on a lightbox or in a window) to maximize the location of the lights and darks. This will never be exact, but get it as close as you can—instant contouring, light and shadow.

It also helps to use the front and back of the same fabric. Unless your fabric is the same on both sides, choosing a fabric that is lighter on the back will give you an instant match in a lighter value. Cut the lips from the front of the fabric as the foundation; then locate the area in your pattern that is lighter and use the back of your fabric in that spot.

Of course, you can use two or three fabrics to show the light, medium, and dark areas of the lips if the value changes are prominent; but unless the lips are large or are a key element in your composition, it is rarely necessary to use more than three fabrics.

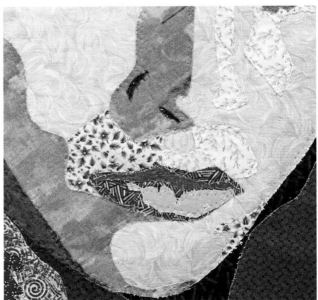

Detail of lips in *Afghan Girl* (full quilt on page 110)

Hands, Arms, and Legs

When a person's hands are a featured element in your quilt, use the same fabrics you used in the face. You may not need as many values, and your hands may even require the addition of a lighter and/or darker value than you used in the face. But since a person's skin is all the same color, you should use the same fabrics for continuity. This is true anywhere skin is visible.

Hands seem tricky, and anyone who has ever taken a drawing class cringes at the thought of drawing hands. But remember, all the information you need is there for you in the pattern, you just need to stay true to what the pattern tells you. Often when cutting the pattern pieces, they just don't look like hands, and this requires a leap of faith. After they are completed, when you step back to view your art quilt, they will look right.

When I made *Old Man* (page 92), *Bittersweet* (page 100), and *Morning Paper* (page 101), I started with the faces. When I liked the way the face looked, I moved to the hands. Since you do not need to create your elements in any particular order, executing the most important element first (the face) followed immediately by the hands (which are the same fabrics) will make the rest of the composition fall into place more easily. It will also allow you to put those fabrics away and move on to use others.

Detail of *Old Man* (full quilt on page 92)

Bittersweet, inspired by a photo by Lin Hsin-Chen

Morning Paper,
inspired by a photo
by Lin Hsin-Chen

Arms and legs, when visible, are no different. Use the same fabrics (going a lighter and/or darker value when needed). A single fabric can sometimes do the trick; often you will need a highlight or shadow, and other times you will want to use multiple fabrics for finer detail and nuance. The level of detail and number of fabrics should be consistent with what is done in the face.

A single fabric can be fussy cut for subtle shadows and highlights on the legs. Detail of *Man Standing Looking at Mountain* (full quilt on page 84).

Two fabrics were used for the legs and arms. Detail of *Pails and Shovels* (full quilt on page 82).

Hair

Whether you are making a small or large quilt, hair can often be effectively made using a single fabric—look at the hair on the boy in *The Boy in the Banyan Tree* and on the women in *Bittersweet* and *In the Moment*. Each is done using a single fabric. The hair in *In the Moment* is cut from a single fabric with little dots in it; I was careful to place the dotted area of the fabric where highlights would be in her hair, framing her face and providing a more detailed image with a single cut of fabric.

The dotted area of fabric is fussy cut to serve as the highlights in her hair. Detail of *In the Moment* (full quilt on page 41).

Adding a second fabric would simply be a function of showing either a highlight or shadowy area and would be approached the same way you would approach any other element with only two fabrics.

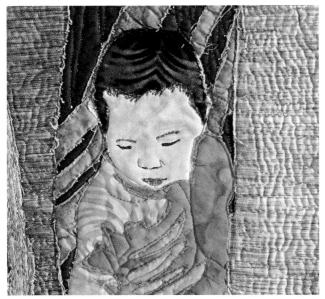

A single fabric is fussy cut for the boy's hair, so the lighter area serves as a highlight. Detail of *The Boy in the Banyan Tree* (full quilt on page 13).

A much more interpretive use of a single dotted fabric that moves from black to white. Detail of *Bittersweet* (full quilt on page 100).

Two fabrics create highlight and shadow areas in the hair. Detail of *Morning Paper* (full quilt on page 101).

When using three fabrics, follow the basic rule of combining light, medium, and dark values. The medium value is the primary hair color and serves as the foundation; the lighter one is the highlight; and the darker is the lowlight or shadow. Here, I don't usually use the back of the medium-value fabric as the light value, because this is where zingers can be used effectively for a lot of visual punch. Look for fabrics with a lot of curving lines, which will translate to a lot of movement.

Hair is another place to have some fun with fabric, and because it does not need to be so realistic, using multiple fabrics can allow you to really let loose and go wild with unexpected fabrics. Start with a foundation—something with little or no pattern that represents the overall color of the hair. Choose several more fabrics with a lot of pattern that vary in value—both lighter and darker—but without a huge jump in value between them, which would cause the hair to look choppy. Zingers are almost required here. Cut soft, curving shapes, one fabric at a time, and lay them onto the foundation so that they are evenly distributed. When you have positioned several fabrics, step back (or take a digital photo) and evaluate. Less is more, and using fewer large cuts of the print fabrics rather than a lot of smaller pieces will look better. Like water and tree bark, using a variety of interesting patterns that "move" in the direction hair would fall will add a lot of energy to the composition.

The hair in *Multifabric Hair* is composed of of seven fabrics (page 33).

Body Language

In an art quilt that shows an entire person (I do a lot of these), body language tells the story. The body language is what allows a viewer to determine the action, what is going on, who these people are, and how they relate to each other.

The good news is that the body language is in the photo. I take a lot of photos wherever I go, and I am always looking for people whose body language will make a good composition and tell an interesting story. Once you have chosen the photo, the body language is simply a matter of following your pattern.

In *Discourse*, the woman and the man are created in one and four fabrics, respectively. Look at the woman with her back to us. With only one fabric (and a little touch of color in her scarf) we can tell that she is a woman and that she is listening intently to the man with her. He is accomplished with only four total fabrics, but we have a very clear picture of what he is doing—the body language is very evident.

Discourse

For *In Her Footsteps*, a single skin tone, a single hair fabric, and only a few variations in their clothing are enough to tell their story. *Man in the Black Track Suit*, *Empty Chair*, and *Shadow Puppets* tell strong stories of the people in them without many fabrics and even without much in the way of background.

In Her Footsteps

Man in the Black Track Suit

Empty Chair

Shadow Puppets

Rush

Photo by Margaret Fox

Of course, depending on the size of your quilt and the level of detail you wish to convey, you can use as many fabrics as you wish. The level of detail does not, however, change the impact of the body language that already exists in the starting photo. In *Rush*, only the silhouettes of the people appear, with bits of color to draw the eye around the composition. The body language is the focal point, and it alone tells the story of the art quilt.

AFGHAN GIRL

Afghan Girl, inspired by a photo by Steve McCurry / Magnum Photos

This art quilt was inspired by Steve McCurry's unforgettable photo *Afghan Girl* (and used with the permission of Steve McCurry / Magnum Photos). For those of you who wish to tackle a more challenging art quilt portrait, the pattern with my drawn lines and the numbered values is provided for you to use along with my instructions. Just remember that the original image is copyrighted, so it can't be shared with the world—it is just for you.

Original photo

Photo by Steve McCurry / Magnum Photos

For greater impact, I cropped the image to focus on her face.

Original GIMP pattern in full color

Pattern in lighter color with traced edges and value numbers

Because of the importance of the eyes, I would not recommend making this in a very small size. The pattern is two sheets of paper wide (horizontally), which makes the small fabric pieces in the eyes a manageable size.

1 Choose the skin tones.

This girl has lovely caramel-colored skin, so you want to look for beige fabrics with that color tone. I have already identified the values for you, as well as the breaks in the placement of the fabrics, to make it easier for you to follow—and you can refer to my finished art quilt (page 110) and close-up of the face (page 114) as guides.

2 Cut out the whole face using value 3 fabric as the foundation.

3 One at a time, cut the other values of the skin tones and place them using a tracing paper template for accuracy. Step back and evaluate, or take a digital image and look at it on your computer, to make sure you like the contours of the face (see Evaluating Your Work, page 58).

4 The eyes are the focal point of this art quilt, so this is where you want to spend some time and attention. What is so amazing about the eyes in the original photo is their color—actually several different colors (see Eyes, page 97).

Choose a white fabric that has a very small-scale print to provide a touch of visual interest without being distracting. The eyes are built in layers: First cut the dark blue fabric that forms the rim of color, followed by the slightly smaller piece of the teal color, followed by the golden center—layering one on top of the others. The black pupil should be placed using your template for accuracy. When the white areas of the light reflection are added, you will really see the eyes come to life.

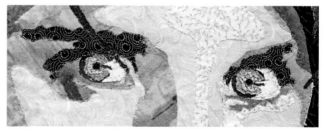

NOTE

Remember to use a tracing paper template to ensure the correct placement of all her facial features.

5 Choose the fabrics for the lips. They can be done in one, two, or more fabrics. I have chosen to use three—a medium base (value 5), one darker fabric for the line that separates the lips (value 8), and a much lighter fabric that is the highlight on the lower lip (value 3)—giving her mouth that beautiful "pouty" look. Again, placement using the tracing paper template will help make your art quilt look like the girl in the photo.

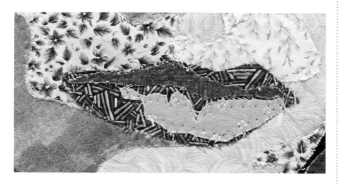

6 Find a dark fabric (value 10) that will serve as the shadow area that blends her face into her hair.

Identify the two fabrics you will use for the hair. One is a dark value 12 foundation and the second is a value 10 highlight. Although both the dark shadow on her face and the highlights in her hair are brown and the same value, I chose to use two different fabrics, so it was clear what was skin and what was hair.

7 The head scarf is a good way to learn to depict the draping of fabric. Choose a medium-value foundation (value 8); then find a light (value 4) and a dark (value 10) that will serve as the highlight and shadow areas in her head scarf.

I have identified three values for the scarf, plus a bit of black. Although in the pattern it appears that a lighter value is on the right, this does not appear in the photo, so I have ignored it.

Draping is organic, like rocks or water, although I follow the pattern as a guide for at least the approximate shape and placement of each highlight and shadow so that it flows. Draping of fabric can look forced and unnatural if not done with gently curving lines and highlights and shadows in the right places.

You do not need to make the head scarf the reddish tone in the original photo; you can choose any color you want—just be sure to stay true to the value numbers.

8 Choose a background fabric. One reason this original photo has such impact is that the background is the complementary color of the scarf (both in a low saturation), making the face more prominent; so if you change the scarf color, you might want to choose a background that is the complement of that color—for example a blue scarf would call for a soft orange background; a purple scarf would benefit from something pale yellow. Look for a background that has an interesting perceived texture, but not a strong print or color that might distract attention from the face.

9 Evaluate at every stage to determine where you might want to make changes. Remember that you are not necessarily looking to make an accurate portrait of this particular person, but to create artwork—so if your art quilt does not look exactly like the girl in the photo, that is okay. Have fun with it and use it as a guide to learn the process.

CONCLUSION

I hope you have found this book helpful in your art quilt journey. Remember, this is just the way I do it, and a lot of other very talented art quilters do things differently. No matter how many books you read or classes or workshops you take, keep in mind that there is no one right way to make an art quilt—and certainly no wrong way. Learn from a lot of people, evaluate what works for you, and disregard the rest. Establish a set of working techniques that fits the way you want to work and that highlights the things you like to do. I don't like making bindings, for instance; you might love that—so do it. I don't like to do a lot of quilting on batting, but that might be your favorite part of the process. Any book or any instructor is only a guide, and after you are pointed in the right direction, you need to find your own path.

The most important advice I can give you is to relax and enjoy the process. There is only one good reason to do something creative; it feeds your soul and brings you pleasure. If you are finding the process stressful, your results will never be as good as they will be if you let go and really have fun—and if it isn't fun, why bother?

Thank you for taking the time to go through this book. The only thing I love more than making art quilts is sharing what I know with others and watching their excitement as the image begins to appear on their worktable. I wish I could come to your house and work directly with you, but I hope this book is the next best thing.

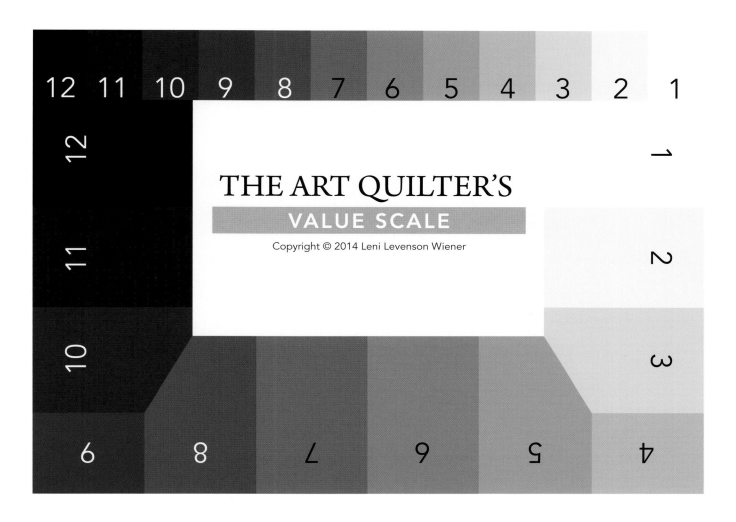

THE ART QUILTER'S
VALUE SCALE

Copyright © 2014 Leni Levenson Wiener

THE ART QUILTER'S

VALUE SCALE

How to Use the Art Quilter's Value Scale

1. Using the side of the card with the gray values, slide the edge of the card from white to black along the area you wish to match; stop where the gray value looks the same as the area you want to match.

2. Use the larger squares on the other three edges of the value scale to double-check your decision.

3. Make a note of that value number.

4. Using the larger squares, choose a fabric in the color you need that matches this value.

You can cut this out of the book and use it, or order a laminated value card from www.leniwiener.com.

ABOUT THE AUTHOR

Leni Levenson Wiener is an art quilter and instructor who has authored three other books on art quilting. Since embarking on her art quilt journey in 2002, her work has been exhibited throughout the United States and internationally and appears in compilation books of art quilts. She regularly contributes articles to the SAQA *Journal* and other quilting magazines.

In addition, Leni is actively involved with SAQA (Studio Art Quilt Associates). She maintains a blog and provides several services via her website, www.leniwiener.com, including assisting emerging artists in finding their voices in a service she calls "art quilt voice coaching," custom-making art quilt patterns, and selling the Art Quilter's Value Scale.

Leni enjoys giving talks and workshops to guilds around the country. She lives just outside New York City with her husband and faithful studio assistant—the little white dog Yendrik (page 87). Her two sons are grown and living in New York.

Great Titles *from* C&T PUBLISHING

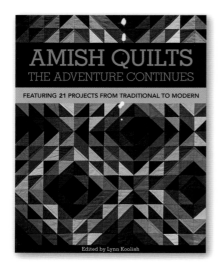
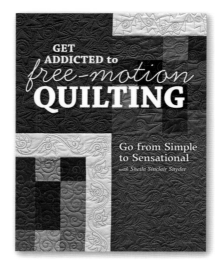
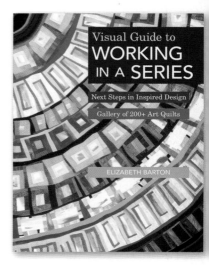

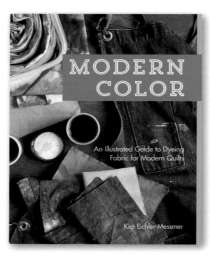

Available at your local retailer or **www.ctpub.com** *or* **800-284-1114**

For a list of other fine books from C&T Publishing, visit our website to view our catalog online.

C&T PUBLISHING, INC.
P.O. Box 1456
Lafayette, CA 94549
800-284-1114

Email: ctinfo@ctpub.com
Website: www.ctpub.com

C&T Publishing's professional photography services are now available to the public. Visit us at www.ctmediaservices.com.

Tips and Techniques can be found at www.ctpub.com > Consumer

For quilting supplies:

COTTON PATCH
1025 Brown Ave.
Lafayette, CA 94549
Store: 925-284-1177
Mail order: 925-283-7883

Email: CottonPa@aol.com
Website: www.quiltusa.com

Note: Fabrics shown may not be currently available, as fabric manufacturers keep most fabrics in print for only a short time.